This Journal Belongs to:

Published by Higgins Publishing
PO Box 1463, Cedar Hill, TX 75106

© 2023-2024 by Sincerely Shanene
sincerelyshanene.com

For ordering information, contact the publisher at HigginsPublishing.com.

All rights reserved. No part of this prayer journal may be reproduced, distributed, or transmitted in any form or by any means, including photocopying, recording, or other electronic or mechanical methods, without the prior written permission of the publisher, except in the case of brief quotations embodied in critical reviews and certain other noncommercial uses permitted
by copyright law.

All Scripture quotations, unless otherwise indicated, are taken from the New King James Version®. Copyright © 1982 by Thomas Nelson, Inc. Used by permission. All rights reserved.

Please be aware that the availability of the Practical Solutions For Financial Needs highlighted throughout this book, are based on the information available at the time of printing. Given the rapid expansion of the internet the implementation of solutions may be subject to change. It's important to note that this information does not constitute financial advice, results can vary, and no guarantees are implied. The content is provided solely for informational purposes. In addition, Higgins Publishing or Sincerely Shanene may receive commission for opportunities presented.

Prayer Journal for Women: 52-Week Financial Breakthrough Scripture Devotional, Journaling Prompts, and Daily Prayers.

_____

This prayer journal is a personal and spiritual tool created to provide encouragement and support.

ISBN: 978-1-941580-99-8 (Full-Color Paperback Edition)

First Edition: April 2024

Dedication

To my three gifts from God,
Tiffany, Douglas & Charlee,
who bring joy to every day of my life.

No temptation has overtaken you except such as is common to man; but God is faithful, who will not allow you to be tempted beyond what you are able, but with the temptation will also make the way of escape, that you may be able to bear it.

1 Corinthians 10:13 (NKJV)

Table of Contents

		Scripture (s)	Introduction	7
Week 1	☐	Phil. 4:19	Divine Assurances of Monetary Prosperity	11
Week 2	☐	2 Cor. 9:6-8	The Principle of Sowing and Reaping	15
Week 3	☐	1 Cor. 4:2	Stewardship and Faithfulness	19
Week 4	☐	2 Tim. 1:7	Breaking the Spirit of Fear	23
Week 5	☐	Prov. 3:13-18	Seeking Wisdom in Finances	27
Week 6	☐	1 Tim. 6:6-8	Contentment in All Circumstances	31
Week 7	☐	Luke 6:38	Generosity and Blessings	35
Week 8	☐	Matt. 6:25-26	God's Provision in Times of Need	39
Week 9	☐	Prov. 22:7	Debt-Free Living	43
Week 10	☐	Mal. 3:10	The Blessings of Tithing	47
Week 11	☐	Prov. 21:5	Financial Planning and Stewardship	51
Week 12	☐	Jer. 29:11	God's Plan for Prosperity	55
Week 13	☐	Psalm 119:105	Finding Strength in God's Word	59
Week 14	☐	Prov. 16:3	God's Guidance in Financial Opportunities	63
Week 15	☐	I Thes. 5:18	A Heart of Thanksgiving	67
Week 16	☐	Joel 2:25-26	Financial Healing and Restoration	71
Week 17	☐	Prov. 14:23	The Blessings of Hard Work	75
Week 18	☐	Prov. 15:22	Seeking Wise Counsel	79
Week 19	☐	2 Cor. 9:7	The Joy of Giving	83
Week 20	☐	Eph. 3:20-21	God's Abundant Blessings	87
Week 21	☐	James. 5:7-8	Importance of Patience	91
Week 22	☐	2 Cor. 5:17	Your Identity in Christ	95
Week 23	☐	Prov. 3:9-10	Financial Wisdom from Proverbs	99
Week 24	☐	2 Cor. 9:10-11	Building a Legacy of Generosity	103
Week 25	☐	Gal. 5:1	Financial Freedom Through Christ	107
Week 26	☐	Gal. 6:7	The Principle of Reaping What You Sow	111
Week 27	☐	Phil. 4:6-7	Overcoming Financial Stress	115

Table of Contents

Week 28	☐	Psalm 100:4-5	Gratitude for Financial Breakthroughs	119
Week 29	☐	Eccl. 3:1	Financial Patience and God's Timing	123
Week 30	☐	Romans 12:2	A Life Transformed	127
Week 31	☐	Prov. 11:25	The Blessing of Generosity	131
Week 32	☐	Hebrews 13:5	Finding Contentment in God's Provision	135
Week 33	☐	2 Cor. 4:18	Faithfulness in Tithing	139
Week 34	☐	Acts 20:35	God's Economy of Abundant Blessings	143
Week 35	☐	Deut. 15:10-11	The Blessing of Openhanded Generosity	147
Week 36	☐	Prov. 16:9	Faithfulness in Financial Planning	151
Week 37	☐	2 Cor. 9:8	God's Boundless Grace and Provision	155
Week 38	☐	Prov. 21:20	Embracing Financial Discipline	159
Week 39	☐	Prov. 3:5-6	Seeking God's Guidance in Financial Decisions	163
Week 40	☐	Luke 14:28-30	Finding Financial Freedom	167
Week 41	☐	1 Tim. 6:17-19	Understanding the Purpose of Wealth	171
Week 42	☐	Matt. 6:24	Financial Alignment and Purpose	175
Week 43	☐	Psalm 34:8	Trusting God in Financial Challenges	179
Week 44	☐	Matt. 25:21	The Joy of Faithfulness	183
Week 45	☐	Matt. 6:19-21	Investing in Eternal Treasures	187
Week 46	☐	Eccl. 4:9	The Blessing of Financial Unity	191
Week 47	☐	Prov. 10:9	Financial Integrity and Honesty	195
Week 48	☐	Prov. 13:22	Generational Blessings and Wise Finances	199
Week 49	☐	Phil. 4:11-13	God's Provision and Strength	203
Week 50	☐	Psalm 34:17-18	Timeless Wisdom and Comfort	207
Week 51	☐	Psalm 23:1	Trusting God in Financial Uncertainty	211
Week 52	☐	Luke 16:10	Financial Accountability and Transparency	215
			Conclusion	219
			Prayer Requests & Answers	221
			About the Author	234
			Free Gift For You	235
			Recommended Reads	236

Introduction

Welcome to the **Prayer Journal for Women** - your 52-week guide to financial breakthrough Scripture devotionals, journaling prompts, and daily prayers.

This journal is crafted to provide spiritual guidance for an abundant life, with intentional repetition throughout the year to instill practical and Biblical financial wisdom. It's important to note that the information shared isn't financial advice but serves as a valuable resource to help provide strength.

Each week, you'll find the following:
- Weekly Scripture(s)
- Bible Verse(s)
- Devotional
- Reflection
- Journaling Prompt
- Life Application
- Daily Prayer
- Closing Prayer
- A Practical Solution for a Financial Need.

Also, there's a Prayer Requests & Answers Section and a carefully chosen collection in the Recommended Reads Section, both tailored to enhance your experience with an extra touch of encouragement.

In addition, the hardcover Keepsake Companion Journal and the spiral Lined Journal await on the next page for you to take additional notes. Consider adding them to your collection for a complete experience with the Floral Medley Collection of the **Prayer Journal for Women.** Your journey to financial well-being begins here.

Sincerely Shanene

More from Sincerely Shanene®

Prayer Journal For Women
Floral Medley Collection
To Enhance Your Devotional Time

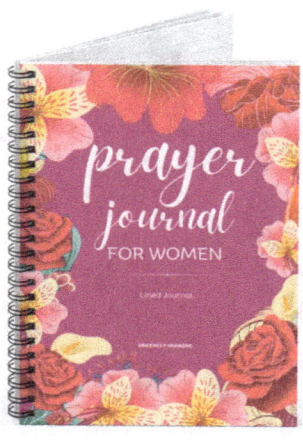

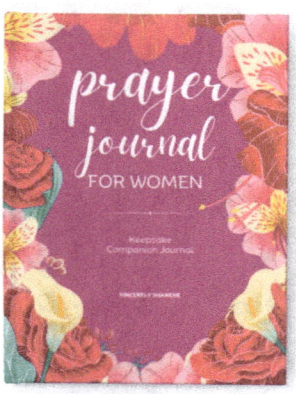

SincerelyShanene.com

Benefits of using this Prayer Journal

This **Prayer Journal for Women** is a resource that will help you with the following:

- Spiritual Growth: This journey will not only transform your financial situation but also deepen your relationship with God. You'll learn to trust Him more fully with every aspect of your life.

- Financial Insight: Through daily Bible readings and thoughtful devotionals, you will gain valuable insights into managing your finances in alignment with God's principles.

- Practical Application: The journaling prompts and life application sections will help you apply what you've learned to your daily life, making your financial goals more achievable.

- Scripture Memorization: Embedding scripture into your financial journey strengthens your spiritual foundation and ignites faith for breakthroughs. By internalizing these truths, you align your mindset with God's promises, fostering resilience and trust amid financial challenges. Let scripture be your beacon of hope and assurance on the path to financial freedom and spiritual growth.

- A Heart of Gratitude: Gratitude is a powerful force, and as you reflect on your blessings daily, you'll cultivate a heart of thankfulness, regardless of your current financial situation.

- Spiritual Community: As you embark on this journey, remember that you are not alone. Many women around the world are seeking financial breakthroughs while deepening their faith, just like you. Connect with a community of like-minded individuals and share your experiences and insights.

A note from the Author

My hope is that, by the end of this 52-Week journey, you will have a clearer understanding of God's purpose for your finances, feel more empowered to take charge of your financial future, and experience the joy of being in alignment with His plan for your life.

So, as you begin, remember that this journey is a partnership between you and God. Be open to the transformation that He wants to work in your life, and trust that He is more than able to provide you with the financial breakthrough you seek.

Explore practical solutions for your financial needs, thoughtfully woven throughout the pages of this journal, tailored for you. These insights are not financial advice but rather gentle guidance to assist you in your pursuit of financial breakthroughs. Embrace them with faith, trusting that they may aid you in exceeding your goals, and ultimately, leaving a lasting legacy of financial abundance.

May this prayer journal be a guide, a source of inspiration, and a place where you can pour out your heart to the Lord as you navigate the path to financial freedom with faith and courage.

Sincerely Shanene

Week 1: Divine Assurances of Monetary Prosperity

Date:

Bible Verse: Philippians 4:19
And my God shall supply all your need according to His riches in glory by Christ Jesus.

Devotional:
The stress of financial matters often weighs on us like a heavy anchor. It's quite common to be enveloped by anxiety related to paying bills, settling debts, and managing mounting daily expenses. However, as we set forth on this exploration, we are anchored by a rock-solid assurance - God's promise to take care of our every necessity.

Our verse for reflection, Philippians 4:19, reaffirms God's role as our ultimate provider. His concern isn't solely for our spiritual growth but also significantly extends to our material and physical necessities. This divine assurance underpins the illustration of God as our benevolent and solicitous Father.

Reflection:
With this verse in your thoughts this week, take some time to ponder the multiple occasions when God has been your provider. Recall those instances when His timely provision was revealed during your moments of dire need.

Daily Prayer
Heavenly Father, grant me discernment in financial matters. Guide me to steward wisely, honoring You with every decision. May I seek Your will above all else, trusting in Your provision and finding peace in Your wisdom.
In Jesus' name, I pray.
Amen.

What is your takeaway from this scripture?

Journaling Prompt: Take a moment to think about a time in your life when God's provision was evident. Perhaps it was a financial breakthrough, an unexpected gift, or a situation where you received exactly what you needed when you needed it. Write down this memory in this journal and express your thankfulness for God's provision.

_____

_____

_____

_____

_____

_____

_____

_____

_____

_____

_____

_____

_____

_____

_____

_____

_____

Life Application: When life tosses curveballs, isn't Philippians 4:19 a wholesome refuge? It's a soothing balm that reassures you in your journey through life's ups and downs. You see, this gem from Scripture is a one-size-fits-all, applicable in pretty much any sticky situation you might find yourself in. It's there, like a faithful friend, ready with a pep talk when you need it.

By being smart about your spendings and keeping faith in God's bounty, is like finding calm in a financial storm. The journey from anxiety to assurance is right there for the taking, all thanks to this profound verse. Just knowing that, feels like a weight lifted, doesn't it?

How can you apply this in your life?

_____
_____
_____
_____
_____
_____
_____
_____
_____
_____
_____
_____

Closing Prayer
Heavenly Father,
I trust in Your abundant provision for all my financial needs. Grant me the wisdom to steward Your blessings well, and may my faith in Your faithful provision grow stronger each day.
In Jesus' name, I pray.
Amen.

Practical Solution for a Financial Need

Seize this Opportunity to Earn Residual Income!

Make up to $800 per referral, when new authors start their author journey!

Week 2: The Principle of Sowing and Reaping

Date:

Bible Reading: 2 Corinthians 9:6-8
But this I say: He who sows sparingly will also reap sparingly, and he who sows bountifully will also reap bountifully. So let each one give as he purposes in his heart, not grudgingly or of necessity; for God loves a cheerful giver. And God is able to make all grace abound toward you, that you, always having all sufficiency in all things, may have an abundance for every good work.

Devotional:
The principle of sowing and reaping is a fundamental concept woven into the fabric of our lives, especially when it comes to finances. In 2 Corinthians 9:6-8, the apostle Paul beautifully illustrates this concept: when you sow generously, you will reap generously. This goes beyond just finances; it applies to the seeds of kindness, love, and generosity you sow into the lives of others.

Reflection:
Imagine a farmer who meticulously sows seeds in a field. If he scatters them sparingly, he will harvest sparingly. But if he sows generously, he will enjoy a bountiful harvest. Likewise, in your financial journey, the generosity and love you extend to others will be multiplied back to you. God loves a cheerful giver, one who gives from the heart, not under compulsion.

Daily Prayer
Heavenly Father, teach me prudence in managing resources. Help me prioritize needs over wants, understanding the value of contentment. Lead me away from the allure of materialism, and let Your truth illuminate my path to financial wisdom.
In Jesus' name, I pray.
Amen.

What is your takeaway from these scriptures?

Journaling Prompt: What areas of your life can you sow into today? Reflect on your life, relationships, and opportunities. Consider where you can sow seeds of kindness, love, generosity, and even financial resources. These acts of giving can be both big and small, and they can extend to your family, friends, community, and even strangers.

_____
_____
_____
_____
_____
_____
_____
_____
_____
_____
_____
_____
_____
_____
_____
_____
_____
_____
_____
_____
_____

Life Application: Give with a cheerful heart, and you will receive abundantly. Today, make a conscious effort to give generously and cheerfully.

It could be a kind word, a helping hand, or a financial gift to someone in need. Be intentional about sowing seeds of love and generosity, and trust that the principle of sowing and reaping will work in your life.

How can you apply this in your life?

_____

_____

_____

_____

_____

_____

_____

_____

_____

_____

_____

_____

_____

Closing Prayer

Heavenly Father, grant me wisdom to steward my finances according to Your divine plan. Help me make decisions aligned with Your will. May my financial journey be a testament to Your guidance, and may I honor You in all aspects of my stewardship.
In Jesus' name, I pray.
Amen

Practical Solution for a Financial Need

Start A Print-On-Demand Business

A print-on-demand business allows for custom designs on popular items like t-shirts, sweatshirts, and mugs with low-risk entry. It eliminates inventory and upfront costs, enabling quick adaptation to market trends. The personalized touch fosters a unique connection between sellers and buyers, enhancing satisfaction and loyalty.

Get Started Today For Free!

Week 3: Stewardship and Faithfulness

Date:

Bible Reading: 1 Corinthians 4:2
Moreover it is required in stewards that one be found faithful.

Devotional:
The concept of stewardship is deeply rooted in the Christian faith. It's the acknowledgment that everything we possess, including our finances, ultimately belongs to God. In 1 Corinthians 4:2, we are reminded of our responsibility as stewards: faithfulness.

Reflection:
As a devoted custodian of God's provisions, we have the sacred duty of prudently and faithfully managing our finances. It's more than just handling wealth; it's a calling to use our financial blessings to glorify God and uplift others. Faithfulness in stewardship involves embodying trustworthiness, responsibility, and accountability, reflecting the virtues cherished in our Christian values. For us, this means aligning our financial decisions with the principles of love, compassion, and grace, ensuring that the resources entrusted to us are utilized in a manner that resonates with our faith and positively contributes to the lives of others.

Daily Prayer
Heavenly Father, instill in me the discipline to budget wisely, acknowledging that all blessings come from You. May I resist the temptation of excessive debt and live within my means. Grant me clarity and diligence as I pursue financial stability. In Jesus' name, I pray. Amen.

What is your takeaway from this scripture?

Journaling Prompt: How can you be a faithful steward of your resources? Take time to reflect on your financial situation. Consider the ways you can be a faithful steward of the resources you've been given. Think about your spending habits, your giving, and your overall financial management. Write down some of your thoughts and goals.

_____
_____
_____
_____
_____
_____
_____
_____
_____
_____
_____
_____
_____
_____
_____
_____
_____
_____
_____

Life Application: Today, commit to being a faithful steward of your finances. It means making wise financial decisions, living within your means, and using your resources in ways that align with God's values. Cultivate a spirit of accountability and gratitude for what you have.

How can you apply this in your life?

_____
_____
_____
_____
_____
_____
_____
_____
_____
_____
_____
_____
_____
_____

Closing Prayer
Heavenly Father,
grant me insight into investments that honor You and benefit others. Help me discern between opportunities that align with Your values and those that lead to greed. May my financial decisions reflect Your kingdom's principles.
In Jesus' name, I pray.
Amen.

Practical Solution for a Financial Need

Homemade Baked Goods or Catering Services

If you have a passion for baking or cooking, consider starting a home-based baking or catering business with a Christian twist. Offer specialty baked goods for events like church gatherings, Bible studies, or fundraisers. Incorporate themes such as scripture-inspired cookies, communion bread, or desserts for Christian holidays. Promote your services through word of mouth, social media, or local community events.

Week 4: Breaking the Spirit of Fear

Date:

Bible Reading: 2 Timothy 1:7
For God has not given us a spirit of fear, but of power and of love and of a sound mind.

Devotional:
Fear and anxiety can often be significant obstacles on the journey to financial freedom. Worries about financial stability, debt, and the future can consume our thoughts, leaving us feeling powerless and anxious. However, 2 Timothy 1:7 reminds us that God has not given us a spirit of fear but of power, love, and a sound mind.

Reflection:
When we anchor ourselves in the power of faith and trust in God, we discover the strength to overcome the paralyzing spirit of fear. By immersing ourselves in God's promises and provision, we not only replace fear and anxiety but also cultivate a profound sense of confidence and clarity of mind. Embracing God's love and power dispels our worries, empowering us to take bold steps towards a financial breakthrough. In this spiritual journey, the assurance of God's guidance becomes a transformative force, allowing us to navigate challenges with resilience and fortitude.

Daily Prayer
Heavenly Father, grant me insight into investments that honor You and benefit others. Help me discern between opportunities that align with Your values and those that lead to greed. May my financial decisions reflect Your kingdom's principles. In Jesus' name, I pray. Amen.

What is your takeaway from this scripture?

Journaling Prompt: What financial fears do you need to overcome? Take some time to identify the specific financial fears that have been holding you back. Whether it's the fear of debt, uncertainty about the future, or other concerns, write them down in your journal. Acknowledging your fears is the first step toward conquering them.

_____
_____
_____
_____
_____
_____
_____
_____
_____
_____
_____
_____
_____
_____
_____
_____
_____

Life Application: Today, make a conscious effort to replace fear with faith and trust in God. Whenever fear or anxiety about your financial situation arises, remind yourself of God's promise in 2 Timothy 1:7. Seek His strength, love, and clarity of mind as you navigate financial challenges.

How can you apply this to your life?

_____
_____
_____
_____
_____
_____
_____
_____
_____
_____
_____
_____
_____

Closing Prayer

Heavenly Father, guide me to opportunities that align with Your plan for my financial prosperity. Grant me discernment in decision-making, and may my actions reflect Your wisdom. Trusting in Your provision, may my journey be a reflection of Your grace and purpose.
In Jesus' name, I pray.
Amen.

Practical Solution for a Financial Need

Free Publishing Guide

Feel the calling to share uplifting and inspiring words through a book? Embrace your purpose with a Free Publishing Guide designed to kickstart your author journey.

Start Your Author Journey Today!

Week 5: Seeking Wisdom in Finances

Date:

Bible Reading: Proverbs 3:13-18
Happy is the man who finds wisdom, and the man who gains understanding; For her proceeds are better than the profits of silver, and her gain than fine gold. She is more precious than rubies, and all the things you may desire cannot compare with her. Length of days is in her right hand, in her left hand riches and honor. Her ways are ways of pleasantness, and all her paths are peace. She is a tree of life to those who take hold of her, and happy are all who retain her.

Devotional:
Financial wisdom is a treasure beyond measure. In Proverbs 3:13-18, we're reminded of the immeasurable worth of wisdom and understanding. It's more profitable than silver, yields better returns than gold, and is more precious than rubies. This wisdom leads to not only financial success but also a life filled with peace, blessings, and honor.

Reflection:
In your journey toward financial breakthrough, seeking wisdom should be a top priority. Wisdom guides you in making sound financial decisions, managing resources effectively, and living with contentment. It leads to a life rich in both spiritual and material blessings.

Daily Prayer
Heavenly Father, grant me patience in times of financial uncertainty. Help me trust in Your timing and providence, knowing that You hold my future in Your hands. Strengthen my faith as I navigate challenges and uncertainties.
In Jesus' name, I pray.
Amen.

What is your takeaway from these scriptures?

Journaling Prompt: How can you seek God's wisdom in your financial decisions? Reflect on the financial decisions you've made in the past. Consider how incorporating God's wisdom could have improved those choices. Then, write down your intentions and strategies for seeking divine wisdom in your financial matters.

_____
_____
_____
_____
_____
_____
_____
_____
_____
_____
_____
_____
_____
_____
_____
_____
_____
_____

Life Application: Today, make a commitment to prioritize seeking God's wisdom in every financial decision you make. This includes budgeting, investments, savings, and even spending. Seek His guidance through prayer, scripture, and wise counsel.

How can you apply this in your life?

_____
_____
_____
_____
_____
_____

Closing Prayer

Heavenly Father,
I trust that Your abundance will overflow in my finances throughout this week. May Your provision surpass my needs, and may my gratitude be a testament to Your boundless grace.
I place my trust in Your unfailing love and providence.
In Jesus' name, I pray.
Amen.

Practical Solution for a Financial Need

Christian Parenting Workshops

Provide workshops and resources for Christian parents, offering guidance on raising children with strong moral and spiritual foundations. Monetize through workshop fees and resource sales.

Recommended Read!

COMPASS by Dr. Ursula Bell
10 Parenting Principles for Guiding Girls Into Becoming Adults

Week 6: Contentment in All Circumstances

Date:

Bible Reading: 1 Timothy 6:6-8
Now godliness with contentment is great gain. For we brought nothing into this world, and it is certain we can carry nothing out. And having food and clothing, with these we shall be content.

Devotional:
Contentment is a treasure that eludes many, especially in a world that often encourages us to pursue more, accumulate possessions, and measure success by material wealth. In 1 Timothy 6:6-8, we are reminded that godliness with contentment is great gain. This passage underscores the truth that our most essential needs are food and clothing, and with these, we should be content.

Reflection:
Contentment is not a call to cease aspirations; instead, it's a state of mind and heart that fosters gratitude for existing blessings. It directs our focus to life's core elements—our relationship with God, connections with loved ones, and inner peace. While ambition propels us forward, contentment ensures appreciation for current joys. Embracing contentment allows us to lead a more purposeful and fulfilling life, appreciating the simplicity and significance of our connections and finding joy in the journey rather than just the destination.

Daily Prayer
Heavenly Father, bless the work of my hands and the fruit of my labor. Help me find fulfillment in honest work and diligence, knowing that it is through Your grace that I am able to provide for myself and others. In Jesus' name, I pray. Amen.

What is your takeaway from these scriptures?

Journaling Prompt: Take a moment to reflect on the blessings in your life, both big and small. Write down the things you're grateful for, even if they're not directly related to your finances. This practice of gratitude can help foster contentment.

_____
_____
_____
_____
_____
_____
_____
_____
_____
_____
_____
_____
_____
_____
_____
_____
_____
_____

Life Application: Today, aim to find contentment in the blessings God has already provided in your life. Recognize that contentment doesn't come from material possessions or wealth but from a heart filled with gratitude for God's provision.

How can you apply this in your life?

_____
_____
_____
_____
_____
_____

Closing Prayer

Heavenly Father,
I surrender my financial worries to You and trust in Your perfect provision. Guide me in making wise choices, and may Your peace fill my heart. I place my faith in Your unfailing love, knowing that You are my provider and source of all abundance.
In Jesus' name, I pray.
Amen.

Practical Solution for a Financial Need

Christian Wellness Coaching

Combine health and spirituality by offering wellness coaching services from a Christian perspective. Provide guidance on healthy living while incorporating biblical principles.

Week 7: Generosity and Blessings

Date:

Bible Reading: Luke 6:38
"Give, and it will be given to you: good measure, pressed down, shaken together, and running over will be put into your bosom. For with the same measure that you use, it will be measured back to you."

Devotional:
Generosity is a core principle in the Christian faith, and it holds profound significance in our financial journey. In Luke 6:38, Jesus encourages us to give, assuring that our generosity will be returned to us in overflowing measure. The principle of generosity is not solely about giving financially but extends to sharing love, kindness, and compassion with others.

Reflection:
Generosity becomes a conduit for God's abundant blessings when we embrace the act of giving. It surpasses transactional exchanges, exuding a reflection of God's character—His inherent generosity. As we mirror His benevolence, we actively participate in His divine plan, inviting blessings that extend beyond material wealth to enrich every facet of our lives.

Daily Prayer
Heavenly Father, grant me wisdom to prioritize generosity in my finances. Help me give cheerfully and sacrificially, knowing that it is more blessed to give than to receive. May my generosity reflect Your love and grace to those in need.
In Jesus' name, I pray.
Amen.

What is your takeaway from this scripture?

Journaling Prompt: Consider your current level of generosity, both in terms of financial giving and in the kindness you extend to others. Reflect on ways you can increase your generosity, whether through your time, resources, or actions. Write down your ideas and intentions in your journal.

___

___

___

___

___

___

___

___

___

___

___

___

___

___

___

___

___

___

___

___

Life Application: Today, practice generosity in your actions, whether it's through a kind word, a helping hand, or a financial gift. Do so with a cheerful heart and the understanding that God's promise in Luke 6:38 will hold true in your life.

How can you apply this in your life?

_____
_____
_____
_____
_____
_____
_____
_____
_____
_____
_____
_____
_____

Closing Prayer
Heavenly Father,
help me remain faithful in my financial journey, knowing You are my ultimate provider. Grant me strength in times of uncertainty, and may my trust in Your guidance grow. As I navigate challenges, let my faith shine as a testament to Your unwavering provision.
In Jesus' name, I pray.
Amen.

Practical Solution for a Financial Need

Christian Counseling or Therapy Services

If you have the qualifications, offer Christian counseling services. This can be done online or in person, providing emotional and spiritual support to those in need.

Week 8: God's Provision in Times of Need

Date:

Bible Reading: Matthew 6:25-26

"Therefore I say to you, do not worry about your life, what you will eat or what you will drink; nor about your body, what you will put on. Is not life more than food and the body more than clothing? Look at the birds of the air, for they neither sow nor reap nor gather into barns; yet your heavenly Father feeds them. Are you not of more value than they?"

Devotional:

In the midst of financial worries and life's challenges, it's easy to lose sight of God's promise to provide for us. Yet, in Matthew 6:25-26, Jesus reminds us of the futility of excessive worry. He asks us to consider the birds of the air and the lilies of the field, which God cares for, and to remember that we are much more valuable in His eyes.

Reflection:

This passage highlights the significance of placing trust in God during challenging times. It urges us to relinquish our anxieties and instead, anchor our faith in His divine provision. By centering our attention on God's unwavering faithfulness, we discover comfort in the assurance that our needs will be met in alignment with His abundant riches and glory.

Daily Prayer

Heavenly Father,
help me cultivate a spirit of gratitude in my financial journey. Teach me to recognize Your blessings, both big and small, and to be thankful for Your provision in all circumstances.
May gratitude shape my attitude towards money and possessions.
In Jesus' name, I pray.
Amen.

What is your takeaway from these scriptures?

Journaling Prompt: Take a moment to recall a specific instance in your life when God's provision was evident. Write down the details of that experience in your journal. This act of remembrance will help reinforce your trust in God's ability to provide.

_____
_____
_____
_____
_____
_____
_____
_____
_____
_____
_____
_____
_____
_____
_____
_____
_____
_____
_____

Life Application: Trust God's provision even when circumstances seem uncertain. Today, commit to trusting God's provision in every aspect of your life, especially in times of need. Release your worries and anxieties and replace them with faith in God's unwavering care for you.

How can you apply this in your life?

_____
_____
_____
_____
_____
_____

Closing Prayer
Heavenly Father,
I trust Your promises of financial abundance to manifest in my life this week. May Your provision exceed my needs, and may I be a conduit of Your blessings to others.
I place my faith in Your unwavering love and provision.
In Jesus' name, I pray.
Amen.

Practical Solution for a Financial Need

Faith-Based Blog or YouTube Channel

Share your insights, teachings, and personal experiences on a blog or YouTube channel. You can monetize through ads, sponsorships, or even by offering exclusive content to subscribers.

Week 9: Debt-Free Living

Date:

Bible Reading: Proverbs 22:7
The rich rule over the poor, and the borrower is slave to the lender.

Devotional:
Debt is a burden that can weigh heavily on our shoulders, affecting not only our financial well-being but also our overall quality of life. In Proverbs 22:7, we are reminded of the enslaving nature of debt. When we owe, we become servants to our lenders, and our financial choices are often dictated by these obligations.

Reflection:
Embarking on the path to financial breakthrough, liberating ourselves from the chains of debt stands as a pivotal stride. This liberation bestows the power to seize command of our financial destiny, make judicious choices, and embrace a more abundant lifestyle. It entails opting for financial freedom, a choice that surmounts the restrictions imposed by debt, paving the way for a future defined by prosperity and wise financial stewardship. In this journey, breaking free from debt is not just a financial decision; it symbolizes a transformative shift towards a life marked by autonomy, responsible choices, and the pursuit of enduring financial well-being.

Daily Prayer
Heavenly Father, grant me humility in times of financial success and prosperity. Keep me mindful of the source of all blessings and guard me against pride and arrogance. Help me use my resources to uplift others and bring glory to Your name.
In Jesus' name, I pray.
Amen.

What is your takeaway from this scripture?

Journaling Prompt: Reflect on your financial goals and your plan to achieve them. Take time to assess your financial goals and the role that debt plays in your life.

What are your objectives for achieving a debt-free existence? What practical steps can you take to make these goals a reality? Write down your thoughts and intentions in your journal.

_____
_____
_____
_____
_____
_____
_____
_____
_____
_____
_____
_____
_____
_____
_____
_____

Life Application: Today, take a step towards becoming debt-free by identifying your existing debts and creating a clear plan for their repayment. This may include budgeting, setting up a debt repayment strategy, and making a commitment to live within your means.

How can you apply this in your life?

_____
_____
_____
_____
_____
_____

Closing Prayer
Heavenly Father, grant me discernment in financial decisions, trusting in Your guidance. Help me make choices aligned with Your will. May my financial journey be a testament to Your wisdom, and may I honor You in all aspects of my stewardship.
In Jesus' name, I pray.
Amen.

_____
_____
_____
_____
_____
_____
_____
_____
_____

Practical Solution for a Financial Need

Christian Songwriting or Music Lessons

If you have musical talent, offer songwriting services with Christian themes. Additionally, provide music lessons either in person or virtually to individuals or groups.

Week 10: The Blessings of Tithing

Date:

Bible Reading: Malachi 3:10
"Bring all the tithes into the storehouse, that there may be food in My house, and try Me now in this," Says the LORD of hosts, "If I will not open for you the windows of heaven and pour out for you such blessing that there will not be room enough to receive it."

Devotional:
Tithing is a spiritual practice that holds profound significance in the Christian faith. It involves giving a portion of your income, typically ten percent, to support the work of God's house and the welfare of others. Malachi 3:10 assures us that when we tithe faithfully, God opens the floodgates of heaven to pour out blessings beyond measure.

Reflection:
Tithing extends beyond mere financial obedience; it embodies an act of trust and faith. It serves as a tangible expression of the belief that God is the ultimate provider. By faithfully tithing, you openly acknowledge His role in your financial affairs, willingly placing them under His care. Tithing becomes a spiritual commitment, affirming your reliance on a divine source and fostering a profound connection between your financial stewardship and your unwavering faith in God's providence.

Daily Prayer
Heavenly Father, guide me in making decisions that honor You with my finances. Lead me in paths of righteousness, helping me to be a good steward of the resources You've entrusted to me. May Your wisdom illuminate every step of my financial journey. In Jesus' name, I pray. Amen.

What is your takeaway from this scripture?

Journaling Prompt: Take a moment to consider your current approach to tithing. Reflect on your attitude and beliefs about this practice. Are there any misconceptions or hesitations you need to address?

_____
_____
_____
_____
_____
_____
_____
_____
_____
_____
_____
_____
_____
_____
_____
_____
_____
_____

Life Application: Today, make a commitment to tithe faithfully and generously. If you are not currently tithing, consider starting this practice as a way to honor God with your finances. Trust in His promise to bless you in ways you cannot fathom.

How can you apply this in your life?

___

Closing Prayer

Heavenly Father,
I trust in Your grace to lead me to financial breakthroughs this week. Guide me with Your wisdom and open doors of opportunity. May Your abundance overflow, and may my faith be a testimony to Your provision.
In Jesus' name, I pray.
Amen.

Practical Solution for a Financial Need

Faith-Infused Cooking Classes

Host virtual or in-person cooking classes that incorporate biblical principles of nourishing the body.
Teach participants how to prepare healthy and spiritually satisfying meals.

Week 11: Financial Planning and Stewardship

Date:

Bible Reading: Proverbs 21:5
The plans of the diligent lead surely to plenty, but those of everyone who is hasty, surely to poverty.

Devotional:
Financial planning is a crucial element of good stewardship. In Proverbs 21:5, we are reminded of the value of diligent planning in achieving financial success. Just as a farmer plans the sowing of seeds for a fruitful harvest, wise financial planning is essential for a prosperous future.

Reflection:
Financial planning encompasses various vital components: establishing clear financial goals, crafting a budget, adeptly managing debt, and making well-informed investment choices. Beyond mere monetary strategy, it stands as an act of stewardship, exemplifying responsibility and wisdom in overseeing the resources entrusted to us by God. This approach extends beyond individual gain, reflecting a commitment to aligning financial decisions with principles of ethical and wise resource management. Through financial planning, we not only secure our financial future but also honor the divine trust placed in us, fostering a sense of accountability and diligence in the thoughtful handling of the blessings we've received.

Daily Prayer
Heavenly Father, grant me clarity in financial planning. Help me set realistic goals and develop strategies to achieve them. May Your wisdom direct my steps, leading me toward financial stability and prosperity.
In Jesus' name, I pray.
Amen.

What is your takeaway from this scripture?

Journaling Prompt: What are your financial goals, and how can you achieve them through planning?

Reflect on your financial goals, whether they involve debt reduction, savings, investments, or charitable giving. Consider how you can achieve these goals and outline a plan in your journal.

_____
_____
_____
_____
_____
_____
_____
_____
_____
_____
_____
_____
_____
_____
_____
_____
_____

Life Application: Take practical steps toward responsible stewardship of your financial resources by exploring both traditional and non-traditional avenues. Alongside budgeting and saving, consider non-traditional approaches like investing in sustainable ventures, or participating in the sharing economy

How can you apply this in your life?

_____
_____
_____
_____
_____
_____

Closing Prayer
Heavenly Father,
I declare my trust in Your plan for financial prosperity to unfold in my life. May Your divine guidance lead me to opportunities, and may my journey be a testament to Your faithfulness. I place my faith in Your abundant provision.
In Jesus' name, I pray.
Amen.

_____
_____
_____
_____
_____
_____
_____
_____

Practical Solution for a Financial Need

Christian Meditation Courses

Develop courses or sessions focusing on Christian meditation and gratefulness. Help others find peace and connection with God through meditating on His Word.

Week 12: God's Plan for Prosperity

Date:

Bible Reading: Jeremiah 29:11
For I know the thoughts that I think toward you, says the LORD, thoughts of peace and not of evil, to give you a future and a hope.

Devotional:
The concept of prosperity is not limited to financial wealth. It encompasses a life that flourishes in all aspects, including spiritual, emotional, and financial well-being. Jeremiah 29:11 reminds us of God's plan for prosperity and a future filled with hope. It is a promise that assures us of His benevolent intentions for our lives.

Reflection:
God's plan for our prosperity emanates from His boundless love and care for us. He envisions our well-being, desiring a future saturated with hope and blessings. It's crucial to recognize that, in His perspective, prosperity extends beyond mere material wealth. While financial abundance is part of it, God's definition encompasses spiritual growth, meaningful relationships, and a life aligned with His purpose. Thus, our pursuit of well-being involves not only financial aspects but also spiritual fulfillment and purposeful living, all orchestrated by God's enduring love and wisdom.

Daily Prayer

Heavenly Father, fill me with wisdom as I navigate financial challenges. Strengthen my resolve to overcome obstacles and persevere with faith. Guide me to solutions that honor You and align with Your purpose for my life.
In Jesus' name, I pray.
Amen.

What is your takeaway from this scripture?

Journaling Prompt: What does prosperity mean to you, and how do you see it aligning with God's plan for your life?

Take time to reflect on your personal definition of prosperity. Consider how it aligns with God's promise in Jeremiah 29:11. Write down your thoughts and aspirations regarding prosperity in your journal.

_____
_____
_____
_____
_____
_____
_____
_____
_____
_____
_____
_____
_____
_____
_____
_____
_____
_____

Life Application: Today, place your trust in God's plan for your prosperity. Acknowledge that He has your best interests at heart and is working for your good. Surrender your financial journey to His guidance and trust in His promise of a future filled with hope.

How can you apply this in your life?

_____
_____
_____
_____
_____
_____
_____
_____
_____
_____
_____
_____

Closing Prayer

Heavenly Father,
I declare my trust in Your plan for financial prosperity to unfold in my life. May Your divine guidance lead me to opportunities, and may my journey be a testament to Your faithfulness.
I place my faith in Your abundant provision.
In Jesus' name, I pray.
Amen.

Practical Solution for a Financial Need

Scripture Memorization Services

Offer personalized scripture memorization plans and coaching. Assist individuals in memorizing verses that are meaningful to them and provide ongoing support.

Week 13: Finding Strength in God's Word

Date:

Bible Reading: Psalm 119:105
Your word is a lamp to my feet and a light to my path.

Devotional:
In the midst of financial challenges, God's Word serves as a guiding light that illuminates our path and provides us with the strength and wisdom we need. Psalm 119:105 beautifully captures the essence of God's Word as a source of guidance and illumination.

Reflection:
The Bible is more than a compilation of stories and verses; it's a timeless source of inspiration, wisdom, and comfort. Amid financial uncertainty, turning to God's Word provides strength, assurance, and the knowledge that we are not alone in our struggles. It reminds us that God's promises are trustworthy, and His guidance is unwavering. In times of economic challenges, the Bible serves as a reliable foundation, offering timeless truths that resonate with enduring wisdom. Its pages become a source of solace and strength, reinforcing the belief that, even in financial uncertainties, the unwavering principles within God's Word provide a steadfast anchor and a guide for navigating life's complexities.

Daily Prayer
Heavenly Father, bless my endeavors to increase income ethically and honorably. Open doors of opportunity and grant me favor in my pursuits. May I use my talents and skills to glorify You and serve others in love.
In Jesus' name, I pray.
Amen.

What is your takeaway from this scripture?

Journaling Prompt: Share a verse from the Bible that has provided you with strength and encouragement during challenging times.

Reflect on a specific Bible verse that has given you strength and encouragement in the face of financial challenges or other difficulties. Write down this verse in your journal and describe how it has impacted your life.

_____
_____
_____
_____
_____
_____
_____
_____
_____
_____
_____
_____
_____
_____
_____
_____
_____

Life Application: Today, take time to immerse yourself in God's Word. Spend time reading, meditating on, and studying passages that offer guidance and strength for your financial journey. Let the wisdom and promises of the Bible renew your spirit.

How can you apply this in your life?

_____

_____

_____

_____

_____

_____

Closing Prayer

Heavenly Father,
I surrender my financial goals to Your will, trusting in Your divine purpose. Guide me in aligning my ambitions with Your plan. May my pursuit be rooted in faith, and may I find fulfillment in the purpose You have ordained for my financial journey.
In Jesus' name, I pray.
Amen.

Practical Solution for a Financial Need

Christian Blogging Consultation

Use your experience to help other Christian bloggers succeed. Offer consulting services where you provide advice on content creation, audience engagement, and monetization strategies.

Week 14: God's Guidance in Financial Opportunities

Date:

Bible Reading: Proverbs 16:3
Commit your works to the LORD, and your thoughts will be established.

Devotional:
Proverbs 16:3 urges us to commit our plans to the Lord, trusting that He will establish them. This principle becomes especially crucial when navigating financial opportunities. Seeking God's guidance in every decision, we acknowledge His sovereignty in our financial journey. This verse instills confidence that as we align our plans with His will, we invite His divine establishment, ensuring that our financial endeavors are guided by His wisdom and orchestrated according to His perfect design.

Reflection:
In the realm of financial opportunities, recognizing the importance of God's guidance and committing our plans to Him becomes a powerful way to align our actions with His will. Proverbs 16:3 stands as a guiding principle, encouraging us to entrust our financial endeavors to the Lord. By doing so, we invite His wisdom and direction into our decision-making, fostering a harmonious relationship between our plans and the divine guidance that leads to financial discernment and success.

Daily Prayer
Heavenly Father, grant me peace amidst financial uncertainty. Help me trust in Your providence and rest in Your promises. May Your presence be my refuge and strength, sustaining me through every trial and tribulation.
In Jesus' name, I pray.
Amen.

What is your takeaway from this scripture?

Journaling Prompt: Reflect on your current approach to financial opportunities. Consider the potential impact of committing your financial plans to God. How might this perspective influence the outcome of your decisions? What practical steps can you take to actively seek God's guidance in financial opportunities? How can you incorporate prayer and discernment into your decision-making process?

Life Application: Think about practical ways to commit your financial plans to the Lord. This might involve intentional prayer, seeking advice from trusted mentors, and aligning your decisions with biblical principles.

How can you apply this in your life?

_____
_____
_____
_____
_____
_____
_____
_____
_____
_____
_____
_____
_____

Closing Prayer

Heavenly Father,
I trust that Your favor will open doors of financial opportunity for me. As I encounter financial opportunities, I commit my plans to You. Guide me in making decisions that align with Your will. May my actions reflect a heart surrendered to Your guidance, trusting that You will establish my plans.
In Jesus' name, I pray.
Amen.

Practical Solution for a Financial Need

Virtual Religious Retreats

Organize and host virtual retreats focused on spiritual growth, mindfulness, and connection with God. Participants can pay to join these transformative experiences from the comfort of their homes.

Week 15: A Heart of Thanksgiving

Date:

Bible Reading: 1 Thessalonians 5:18
In everything give thanks; for this is the will of God in Christ Jesus for you.

Devotional:
Gratitude is a transformative attitude that can change how we perceive our financial circumstances. In 1 Thessalonians 5:18, we are instructed to give thanks in all circumstances. This verse reminds us that gratitude is not contingent on our circumstances but is a choice we can make daily.

Reflection:
In times of financial hardship, it's natural to dwell on scarcity rather than abundance. Yet, fostering a spirit of thanksgiving can alter our outlook. Gratitude prompts us to recognize the blessings, be they substantial or modest, fostering contentment and revealing the goodness of God even amid challenges. By shifting our focus from what we lack to what we possess, gratitude becomes a powerful force, enabling us to navigate tough circumstances with a renewed perspective and an acknowledgment of the inherent goodness that persists, even in difficult financial situations.

Daily Prayer
Heavenly Father, grant me discernment in financial partnerships and ventures. Protect me from schemes and enticements that lead astray. Lead me to opportunities that align with Your will and bring honor to Your name.
In Jesus' name, I pray.
Amen.

What is your takeaway from this scripture?

Journaling Prompt: Take a moment to list three things you're thankful for today. These can be related to your financial situation or other aspects of your life. Express gratitude for the positive elements, no matter how small they may seem.

_____
_____
_____
_____
_____
_____
_____
_____
_____
_____
_____
_____
_____
_____
_____
_____
_____
_____

Life Application: Today, make a commitment to practice daily gratitude. Take time each day to reflect on the blessings in your life, no matter how challenging your financial circumstances may be. Cultivate a heart of thanksgiving in all situations.

How can you apply this in your life?

_____
_____
_____
_____
_____
_____
_____
_____
_____
_____
_____
_____
_____

Closing Prayer

Heavenly Father,
I rely on Your promises for financial provision and prosperity this week. I'm grateful for Your blessings despite financial challenges. Help me maintain a thankful heart. Grant grace to find reasons for gratitude daily, bringing peace and contentment to my financial journey. Guide me, and may my trust in You deepen.
In Jesus' name, I pray.
Amen.

Practical Solution for a Financial Need

Christian Graphic Design Services

Offer graphic design services with a Christian flair. Create custom designs for churches, ministries, or individuals looking to incorporate faith-based elements into their branding and materials.

Week 16: Financial Healing and Restoration

Date:

Bible Reading: Joel 2:25-26
"So I will restore to you the years that the swarming locust has eaten, the crawling locust, the consuming locust, and the chewing locust, my great army which I sent among you. You shall eat in plenty and be satisfied, and praise the name of the LORD your God, who has dealt wondrously with you; and My people shall never be put to shame."

Devotional:
Financial challenges can often feel like they've devoured our resources and opportunities. Yet, Joel 2:25-26 offers a profound message of hope and restoration. It speaks of God's ability to restore what has been lost, even after years of difficulty.

Reflection:
In your financial journey, keep in mind that God is adept at healing and restoration. He has the capacity to reclaim lost years and bestow abundance upon you. This commitment goes beyond material wealth, encompassing the restoration of your confidence, peace of mind, and faith in His providence. Trusting in God's ability to bring about healing and renewal allows for a comprehensive sense of recovery, not limited to financial aspects but extending to the restoration of inner strength, mental peace, and a fortified belief in His sustaining providence throughout your financial journey.

Daily Prayer
Heavenly Father, help me break free from financial bondage and debt. Provide strategies and resources to overcome financial burdens. Grant me wisdom to manage my resources wisely and live a life of financial freedom. In Jesus' name, I pray. Amen.

What is your takeaway from these scriptures?

Journaling Prompt: Take time to reflect on specific areas in your financial life that require healing and restoration. These may include debt, lost opportunities, or broken financial relationships. Write down your reflections in your journal.

_____
_____
_____
_____
_____
_____
_____
_____
_____
_____
_____
_____
_____
_____
_____
_____
_____

Life Application: Today, make a commitment to trust in God's promise of restoration. Ask for His guidance in healing and rebuilding the areas in your financial life that need attention. Believe that, with His help, your financial situation can experience renewal and abundance.

How can you apply this in your life?

_____
_____
_____
_____
_____
_____
_____
_____
_____
_____
_____
_____
_____

> **Closing Prayer**
> Heavenly Father,
> I trust in Your wisdom to navigate financial challenges with grace and faith. I trust in Your promise of financial healing. Thank You for redeeming past difficulties. Grant me grace and guidance as I rebuild, experiencing abundance on this financial journey.
> In Jesus' name, I pray.
> Amen.

Practical Solution for a Financial Need

Online Christian Book Club

Start an online book club focused on Christian literature. Charge a membership fee and facilitate discussions, providing a platform for readers to engage in meaningful conversations about faith-inspired books.

Check out the Recommended Reads Section on page 236 to help you get started.

Week 17: The Blessings of Hard Work

Date:

Bible Reading: Proverbs 14:23
In all labor there is profit, but idle chatter leads only to poverty.

Devotional:
Hard work is a timeless principle that transcends financial matters. In Proverbs 14:23, we are reminded that diligent and consistent effort leads to profit and success. It's a message that encourages us to take action and put in the work necessary to achieve our goals.

Reflection:
In the pursuit of financial breakthrough, hard work stands as a crucial element. While prayer seeks God's provision, it often materializes as opportunities that necessitate commitment and diligence. Our active engagement and dedicated efforts play a pivotal role in the process of financial growth. The blessings of hard work underscore that alongside divine guidance, our commitment is instrumental in seizing opportunities and achieving desired financial advancement. This synergy emphasizes that financial breakthroughs are not solely reliant on prayer; they involve active participation, recognizing the reciprocal relationship between our endeavors and God's provisions. Through a blend of faith and industrious efforts, we navigate the path toward financial prosperity with a deeper understanding of the role both play in this transformative journey.

Daily Prayer

Heavenly Father, cultivate in me a heart of generosity and compassion. Help me recognize the needs of others and respond with love and generosity. Use me as a vessel of Your grace and provision in the lives of those around me.

In Jesus' name, I pray.

Amen.

What is your takeaway from this scripture?

Journaling Prompt: Take time to reflect on your financial goals and aspirations. Consider the areas where you can put in more effort, be more diligent, or work smarter. Write down your thoughts and intentions in your journal.

Life Application: Today, make a commitment to embrace the value of hard work in your financial journey. Be diligent in your work, whether it's related to your career, financial planning, or personal investments. Recognize that your efforts are part of God's provision for your financial prosperity.

How can you apply this in your life?

_____
_____
_____
_____
_____
_____
_____
_____
_____
_____
_____
_____
_____

> **Closing Prayer**
> Heavenly Father,
> I place my financial burdens at Your feet, trusting in Your strength. Grant me guidance and strength to value hard work in my financial pursuits. Bestow diligence and wisdom to work smarter.
> In my efforts, may Your provision lead me to achieve financial goals.
> In Jesus' name, I pray.
> Amen.

Practical Solution for a Financial Need

Virtual Bible Journaling Workshops

Host virtual workshops on Bible journaling, teaching participants creative ways to engage with scripture through art. Charge a membership fee for access to these interactive and inspirational sessions.

Week 18: Seeking Wise Counsel

Date:

Bible Reading: Proverbs 15:22
Without counsel, plans go awry, but in the multitude of counselors they are established.

Devotional:
Making financial decisions can be challenging, and seeking wise counsel is a biblical principle that can significantly impact your financial journey. In Proverbs 15:22, we're reminded that without counsel, plans often fail, but with the guidance of many advisers, they are more likely to succeed.

Reflection:
Seeking wise counsel isn't an admission of personal irresponsibility but a recognition of the importance of tapping into the experience and wisdom of others. Whether from financial advisors, mentors, or trusted friends, seeking counsel offers valuable insights, alternative perspectives, and aids in making informed decisions. It's a pragmatic approach, acknowledging that leveraging the knowledge and experience of others is a wise and strategic move, enhancing one's ability to navigate challenges and make well-informed choices without diminishing personal responsibility. The counsel received becomes a valuable tool, augmenting individual judgment and contributing to a more robust decision-making process in various aspects of life, including financial matters.

Daily Prayer
Heavenly Father, grant me the strength to resist the lure of materialism and worldly desires. Help me find contentment in You alone, knowing that true wealth is found in Your presence. May I seek first Your kingdom and righteousness in all things.
In Jesus' name, I pray.
Amen.

What is your takeaway from this scripture?

Journaling Prompt: Recall a specific instance in your life when seeking wise counsel played a role in making a sound financial decision. Reflect on how the advice you received impacted the outcome. Write down your reflections in your journal.

_____
_____
_____
_____
_____
_____
_____
_____
_____
_____
_____
_____
_____
_____
_____
_____
_____
_____
_____
_____

Life Application: Today, make a commitment to be intentional about seeking wise counsel in your financial matters. Identify areas where you could benefit from advice or guidance, and reach out to individuals who possess the knowledge and experience to assist you in making informed choices.

How can you apply this in your life?

_____
_____
_____
_____
_____
_____
_____
_____
_____
_____
_____
_____
_____
_____

Closing Prayer

Heavenly Father, guide me in seeking and heeding wise counsel. Grant discernment in choosing the right advisers, and instill humility to accept their guidance. By seeking wisdom, may I position myself for financial success and spiritual growth.
In Jesus' name, I pray.
Amen.

Practical Solution for a Financial Need

Christian Comedy or Storytelling

If you have a talent for humor or storytelling, consider performing Christian comedy or storytelling at events, conferences, or online platforms. Monetize through ticket sales or virtual tips.

Week 19: The Joy of Giving

Date:

Bible Reading: 2 Corinthians 9:7
So let each one give as he purposes in his heart, not grudgingly or of necessity; for God loves a cheerful giver.

Devotional:
The act of giving holds profound spiritual significance in the Christian faith. In 2 Corinthians 9:7, we're reminded that giving should be a matter of the heart, driven by a joyful spirit rather than reluctance or compulsion. The joy of giving is not only about financial generosity but also a reflection of the love and grace we have received from God.

Reflection:
Giving isn't merely an act benefiting the recipient; it brings joy to the giver as well. It stands as a powerful expression of gratitude, obedience, and love. When we give with a cheerful heart, we align ourselves with God's character, as He is the ultimate giver. This act of generosity not only blesses others but also contributes to the enrichment of our own spiritual journey, fostering a deeper sense of fulfillment and connection with the principles of gratitude and selflessness. The joy experienced in giving extends beyond the material realm, leaving an enduring impact on both the giver and the recipient.

Daily Prayer
Heavenly Father,
fill me with gratitude for Your abundant blessings. Help me see Your hand at work in every aspect of my life, including my finances. May thankfulness overflow from my heart as I acknowledge Your goodness and faithfulness. In Jesus' name, I pray.
Amen.

What is your takeaway from this scripture?

Journaling Prompt: Recall a specific moment in your life when you experienced the joy of giving, whether through financial generosity, acts of kindness, or service to others. Reflect on the emotions and impact of that experience. Write down your thoughts in your journal.

Life Application: Today, make a commitment to practice the joy of giving in your financial and daily life. Seek opportunities to give generously, whether it's through financial donations, acts of kindness, or supporting charitable causes. Embrace the delight that comes from giving with a cheerful heart.

How can you apply this in your life?

_____
_____
_____
_____
_____
_____
_____
_____
_____
_____
_____
_____
_____

Closing Prayer

Heavenly Father, grant me guidance and a heart that delights in giving. Make me a cheerful giver, seeking opportunities to bless others. As I give joyfully, align my heart with Yours and fulfill Your purpose.
In Jesus' name, I pray.
Amen.

Practical Solution for a Financial Need

Faith-Based Language Learning

Teach a language, incorporating Christian teachings and Biblical stories into the curriculum. Offer classes online or in person, providing a unique and faith-centered approach to language education.

Week 20: God's Abundant Blessings

Date:

Bible Reading: Ephesians 3:20-21
Now to Him who is able to do exceedingly abundantly above all that we ask or think, according to the power that works in us, to Him be glory in the church by Christ Jesus to all generations, forever and ever. Amen.

Devotional:
Ephesians 3:20 reminds us of the extravagant generosity of God. He is not limited by our expectations or imagination; His ability to bless us knows no bounds. God's blessings are not always confined to the material or financial; they extend to every aspect of our lives, including spiritual, emotional, and relational blessings.

Reflection:
In the pursuit of financial breakthrough and prosperity, it's vital to acknowledge that God's blessings often exceed our comprehension. Placing trust in Him and aligning our desires with His will can result in abundant provision, surpassing what we might request or even fathom. This verse serves as a testimony to the boundless nature of God's blessings, emphasizing the potential for unexpected and unparalleled abundance when we anchor our aspirations in faith and align them with His divine purpose. It underscores the notion that, in the realm of God's blessings, there exists a vast reservoir of abundance beyond the scope of our finite understanding.

Daily Prayer
Heavenly Father, grant me wisdom to invest in Kingdom priorities.
Help me use my resources to advance Your kingdom on earth and make an eternal impact.
May my financial decisions reflect Your values and contribute to Your purposes.
In Jesus' name, I pray.
Amen.

What is your takeaway from these scriptures?

Journaling Prompt: Recall a specific instance when you experienced God's abundant blessings in your life. Reflect on the circumstances and the emotions associated with that experience. Write down your reflections in your journal.

_____
_____
_____
_____
_____
_____
_____
_____
_____
_____
_____
_____
_____
_____
_____
_____
_____
_____
_____
_____
_____

Life Application: Today, make a commitment to trust in God's ability to provide abundantly in your financial journey. Seek His guidance, align your desires with His will, and remain open to the limitless blessings He can bestow upon you.

How can you apply this in your life?

_____

_____

_____

_____

_____

_____

Closing Prayer

Heavenly Father,
I trust in Your power to provide beyond imagination. Thank You for abundant blessings. Grant me unwavering faith to trust Your limitless provision in my financial journey. Your blessings are immeasurable, and I place my trust in Your boundless grace.
In Jesus' name, I pray.
Amen.

Practical Solution for a Financial Need

Christian Wedding Officiant Services

Become a licensed wedding officiant and offer Christian wedding ceremonies. Provide a personalized and faith-centered experience for couples, charging fees for your services.

Week 21: Importance of Patience

Date:

Bible Reading: James 5:7-8
Therefore be patient, brethren, until the coming of the Lord. See how the farmer waits for the precious fruit of the earth, waiting patiently for it until it receives the early and latter rain. You also be patient. Establish your hearts, for the coming of the Lord is at hand.

Devotional:
Patience is a virtue that plays a significant role in our financial journey. In James 5:7-8, we are encouraged to be patient, much like a farmer patiently waits for the harvest. Patience is not merely the ability to wait, but the capacity to maintain a positive attitude and persevere during challenging times.

Reflection:
Financial breakthroughs seldom occur overnight, and establishing stability often demands prolonged effort. Embracing patience becomes imperative, enabling steadfastness and trust in God's timing. It serves as a deterrent against impulsive financial decisions, fostering resilience during uncertain periods. Patience isn't passive waiting but an active trust that aligns our actions with an enduring belief in God's providence.

Daily Prayer
Heavenly Father, grant me wisdom in budgeting and spending. Help me prioritize needs over wants and exercise self-control in financial matters. May I honor You with every dollar entrusted to me and find satisfaction in Your provision.
In Jesus' name, I pray.
Amen.

What is your takeaway from these scriptures?

Journaling Prompt: Take time to reflect on your financial journey and the role of patience. Consider how patience has impacted your financial decisions and outcomes. Write down your thoughts in your journal.

_____
_____
_____
_____
_____
_____
_____
_____
_____
_____
_____
_____
_____
_____
_____
_____
_____
_____
_____

Life Application: Today, make a commitment to practice patience in your financial decisions. Before making major financial choices, take time to reflect, seek wise counsel, and trust in God's timing. Patience can lead to better, more considered financial decisions.

How can you apply this in your life?

_____
_____
_____
_____
_____
_____
_____
_____
_____
_____
_____
_____
_____

Closing Prayer
Heavenly Father, grant me patience in my financial journey. Help me trust Your timing, remaining steadfast in times of waiting and uncertainty.
Your plan unfolds perfectly, and I rely on Your guidance.
In Jesus' name, I pray.
Amen.

Practical Solution for a Financial Need

Virtual Women's Bible Study Groups

Create and lead virtual Bible study groups specifically for women. Charge a membership fee and provide a platform for deep spiritual discussions and connections.

Week 22: Your Identity in Christ

Date:

Bible Reading: 2 Corinthians 5:17
Therefore, if anyone is in Christ, he is a new creation; old things have passed away; behold, all things have become new.

Devotional:
Your identity in Christ is foundational to your financial journey. In 2 Corinthians 5:17, we're reminded that when we are in Christ, we become new creations. Our identity is no longer defined by the standards of the world but by the love, grace, and purpose found in Christ.

Reflection:
Comprehending your identity in Christ brings liberation. It entails acknowledging that your worth and significance transcend financial status or accomplishments. Your genuine identity is that of a beloved child of God, inherently valuable, purposeful, and holding a unique place in His plan. This understanding emancipates you from the constraints of societal measures of success, affirming that your true worth is rooted in your divine relationship rather than external achievements. Recognizing this liberating truth empowers a profound sense of self-worth, providing a solid foundation that transcends the transient nature of material success, anchoring your identity in the enduring truth of your cherished status as a child of God.

Daily Prayer
Heavenly Father, guide me in seeking opportunities to increase my financial literacy. Help me educate myself on wise money management practices and develop skills for financial success. Empower me to make informed decisions that align with Your will. In Jesus' name, I pray. Amen.

What is your takeaway from this scripture?

Journaling Prompt: Take time to reflect on your identity in Christ. Consider how this understanding affects your financial perspective. How does recognizing your true identity influence your financial goals, decisions, and attitudes? Write down your reflections in your journal.

_____
_____
_____
_____
_____
_____
_____
_____
_____
_____
_____
_____
_____
_____
_____
_____
_____
_____
_____

Life Application: Today, make a commitment to base your financial decisions on your identity in Christ. Recognize your worth in Him and seek to align your financial choices with His values, principles, and purpose for your life.

How can you apply this in your life?

_____
_____
_____
_____
_____
_____
_____
_____
_____
_____
_____
_____
_____
_____
_____

Closing Prayer

Heavenly Father, guide me in embracing my true identity in Christ. May I live in alignment with Your values and seek Your guidance in financial decisions. As I honor my identity in You, ground my financial journey in Your wisdom and purpose.
In Jesus' name, I pray.
Amen.

Practical Solution for a Financial Need

Christian Travel Planning Services

Combine a love for travel with faith by offering travel planning services for individuals or groups looking for Christian-themed travel experiences. Plan trips to historical religious sites or organize faith-based retreats.

Week 23: Financial Wisdom from Proverbs

Date:

Bible Reading: Proverbs 3:9-10
Honor the LORD with your possessions, and with the firstfruits of all your increase; so your barns will be filled with plenty, and your vats will overflow with new wine.

Devotional:
The book of Proverbs is a treasure trove of financial wisdom. Proverbs 3:9-10 emphasizes the importance of honoring the Lord with your wealth by giving your first fruits. This practice reflects the principle of giving back to God and trusting that He will bless you abundantly.

Reflection:
Proverbs offers practical guidance on financial matters, advising on diligence, generosity, stewardship, and debt avoidance. Implementing these principles in your financial life can pave the way for prosperity, peace, and wise decision-making. The wisdom found in Proverbs provides timeless insights, emphasizing the importance of hard work, responsible financial management, and generosity. By adhering to these principles, you can navigate their financial journey with prudence and discernment, cultivating a stable and prosperous life.

Daily Prayer
Heavenly Father, bless my efforts to save and invest for the future. Help me be diligent in setting aside resources for unexpected expenses and long-term goals. May I be a good steward of Your blessings and use them wisely.
In Jesus' name, I pray.
Amen.

What is your takeaway from these scriptures?

Journaling Prompt: Consider a Proverb from the book of Proverbs that has significantly influenced your financial decisions. Reflect on the impact it has had on your financial choices and the outcomes you've experienced. Write down your thoughts in your journal.

Life Application: Today, make a commitment to apply the financial wisdom found in Proverbs to your daily life. Identify areas in your financial journey where these principles can be implemented and start making changes accordingly.

How can you apply this in your life?

_____
_____
_____
_____
_____
_____
_____
_____
_____
_____
_____
_____
_____

Closing Prayer
Heavenly Father, grant me wisdom to apply financial principles from Proverbs. Guide me in honoring You with my wealth, being a wise steward, and making sound choices. As I apply these principles, may I experience the blessings of financial wisdom.
In Jesus' name, I pray.
Amen.

Practical Solution for a Financial Need

Christian Wedding Planning Services

Specialize in planning Christian weddings, ensuring
that every aspect of the ceremony reflects the couple's faith.
Offer services such as venue selection,
decor planning, and coordination on the big day.

Week 24: Building a Legacy of Generosity

Date:

Bible Reading: 2 Corinthians 9:10-11
Now may He who supplies seed to the sower, and bread for food, supply and multiply the seed you have sown and increase the fruits of your righteousness, while you are enriched in everything for all liberality, which causes thanksgiving through us to God.

Devotional:
Building a legacy of generosity is a profound way to leave a lasting impact. In 2 Corinthians 9:11, we learn that as we are enriched in every way, we have the opportunity to be generous on every occasion. Our acts of generosity not only bless others but also lead to thanksgiving to God, who is the ultimate source of all we have.

Reflection:
Generosity has the potential to craft a lasting legacy that endures beyond our lifetimes. It mirrors a heart brimming with love and compassion, imprinting a positive influence on the world. Through selfless and abundant giving, we become inspirations for others, encouraging the perpetuation of a legacy characterized by love and care. This ripple effect, initiated by our generosity, extends the impact, fostering a culture of compassion that outlasts individual lifespans and contributes to a collective legacy of benevolence and kindness.

Daily Prayer
Heavenly Father, grant me patience as I wait for financial breakthroughs. Help me trust Your timing and remain steadfast in prayer. Strengthen my faith to believe in Your promises and persevere through challenges.
In Jesus' name, I pray.
Amen.

What is your takeaway from these scriptures?

Journaling Prompt: Take a moment to reflect on the kind of legacy you desire to leave through generosity. Consider how you want to be remembered and how your acts of generosity can impact future generations. Write down your thoughts in your journal.

Life Application: Today, make a commitment to practice generosity in your daily life and financial decisions. Look for opportunities to bless others with your resources, time, and love. Seek to build a legacy of generosity that extends to those around you.

How can you apply this in your life?

_____
_____
_____
_____
_____
_____

Closing Prayer

Heavenly Father, guide and strengthen me to build a legacy of generosity. May my acts of love and kindness bless others and inspire future generations. In practicing generosity, may I fulfill a higher purpose, leaving a lasting legacy of Your love and grace. In Jesus' name, I pray. Amen.

_____
_____
_____
_____
_____
_____
_____
_____

Practical Solution for a Financial Need

Christian Freelance Editing Services

Provide freelance editing services specifically for Christian authors, bloggers, or organizations. Help polish and refine content while ensuring it aligns with Christian values.

Week 25: Financial Freedom Through Christ

Date:

Bible Reading: Galatians 5:1
Stand fast therefore in the liberty by which Christ has made us free, and do not be entangled again with a yoke of bondage.

Devotional:
True financial freedom goes beyond having wealth; it is about being released from the bondage of financial worry, fear, and debt. In Galatians 5:1, we're reminded that Christ's sacrifice has set us free, and we are encouraged to stand firm in that freedom.

Reflection:
Financial freedom through Christ involves trusting in His provision, surrendering financial burdens, and finding peace and contentment irrespective of circumstances. It's recognizing that our worth isn't defined by possessions but by our identity in Christ—an aspect worth remembering. This acknowledgment emphasizes the importance of constantly keeping this truth in mind, steering away from a mindset that equates possessions with self-worth. By anchoring our understanding of financial freedom in Christ, we establish a resilient foundation that isn't contingent on material abundance, fostering enduring peace and contentment regardless of the fluctuations in our financial situations. This is something that we must always keep in remembrance.

Daily Prayer
Heavenly Father, protect me from the temptation of financial shortcuts and unethical practices. Help me uphold integrity and honesty in all my financial dealings. May I be a beacon of light in a world of darkness, reflecting Your righteousness.
In Jesus' name, I pray.
Amen.

What is your takeaway from this scripture?

Journaling Prompt: Take a moment to reflect on the concept of financial freedom through Christ. Consider the areas of your financial life where you still feel burdened and how you can apply the freedom Christ offers. Write down your thoughts in your journal.

_____
_____
_____
_____
_____
_____
_____
_____
_____
_____
_____
_____
_____
_____
_____
_____
_____
_____
_____

Life Application: Today, make a commitment to surrender your financial worries to Christ. Trust in His provision, seek His guidance in your financial decisions, and stand firm in the freedom He offers. Financial freedom through Christ is not about the absence of financial challenges but about finding peace and confidence in His care.

How can you apply this in your life?

_____
_____
_____
_____
_____
_____
_____
_____
_____
_____
_____
_____
_____

Closing Prayer
Heavenly Father,
grant me strength to find financial freedom through Christ. Help me stand firm
in Your provision, trusting Your guidance. Release me from financial burdens and fears. In Christ, I find true freedom.
In Jesus' name, I pray.
Amen.

Practical Solution for a Financial Need

Online Christian Bookstore

Create an online bookstore specializing in Christian literature. Offer a curated selection of books, devotionals, and resources, and monetize through book sales and affiliate marketing.

Week 26: The Principle of Reaping What You Sow

Date:

Bible Reading: Galatians 6:7
Do not be deceived, God is not mocked; for whatever a man sows, that he will also reap.

Devotional:
The principle of reaping what you sow is a foundational concept in the Bible. Galatians 6:7 serves as a reminder that our actions and decisions have consequences, both in our spiritual and financial lives. Just as a farmer's harvest is determined by the seeds he sows, our financial outcomes are influenced by the choices we make.

Reflection:
This principle urges mindfulness in financial decisions, understanding that generosity, prudent stewardship, and responsible planning yield blessings and prosperity. Conversely, poor choices and selfishness can lead to difficulties. It's a call to intentionally sow seeds of faith, wisdom, and love in our financial journey, emphasizing the significance of purposeful actions aligned with enduring values. Recognizing the cause-and-effect nature of financial choices underscores the importance of cultivating a mindset that prioritizes wise decisions and selflessness. This intentional approach to financial stewardship establishes a framework for enduring prosperity, aligning actions with values that foster both personal and collective well-being.

Daily Prayer
Heavenly Father, surround me with wise counsel and mentorship in financial matters. Help me seek guidance from those who align with Your principles and can offer sound advice. May I humbly receive wisdom and apply it to my life.
In Jesus' name, I pray.
Amen.

What is your takeaway from this scripture?

Journaling Prompt: Take time to reflect on the principle of reaping what you sow in your financial life. Consider the financial choices and decisions you've made and how they may have impacted your current situation. Write down your reflections in your journal.

_____
_____
_____
_____
_____
_____
_____
_____
_____
_____
_____
_____
_____
_____
_____
_____
_____
_____

Life Application: Today, make a commitment to make intentional financial choices aligned with God's principles. Seek to sow seeds of generosity, wise stewardship, and love in your financial journey. Trust that by sowing with intention, you will reap the blessings God has in store for you.

How can you apply this in your life?

_____
_____
_____
_____
_____
_____
_____
_____
_____
_____
_____
_____
_____

Closing Prayer

Heavenly Father, guide me in sowing seeds of faith and love in my financial journey. May my choices align with Your principles. As I do so, grant me the blessings of reaping what I sow in both my spiritual and financial life.
In Jesus' name, I pray.
Amen.

Practical Solution for a Financial Need

Christian Subscription Box for Kids

Create a subscription box tailored to children, filled with Christian-themed books, activities, and educational materials. Parents can subscribe to receive these boxes monthly for their kids.

Week 27: Overcoming Financial Stress

Date:

Bible Reading: Philippians 4:6-7
Be anxious for nothing, but in everything by prayer and supplication, with thanksgiving, let your requests be made known to God; and the peace of God, which surpasses all understanding, will guard your hearts and minds through Christ Jesus.

Devotional:
Financial stress is a common challenge, but the Bible offers guidance on overcoming it. Philippians 4:6-7 reminds us not to be anxious but to present our concerns to God through prayer and thanksgiving. The promise is that God's peace, which surpasses human understanding, will guard our hearts and minds.

Reflection:
Overcoming financial stress starts with trusting God's provision and seeking His guidance. Approaching financial challenges with faith and prayer offers a pathway to finding peace amid stress. It's a practical and grounded approach, emphasizing the importance of strategic financial planning, resource management, and seeking assistance when required. By intertwining faith with practical steps, individuals can navigate financial stress with a balanced perspective, acknowledging the role of both trust in God's guidance and practical financial management in cultivating lasting peace in the midst of challenges.

Daily Prayer
Heavenly Father,
grant me resilience in times of financial setbacks and disappointments.
Help me learn from mistakes and grow stronger in faith.
May Your grace sustain me through hardships, knowing that You work all things for good.
In Jesus' name, I pray.
Amen.

What is your takeaway from these scriptures?

Journaling Prompt: Recall a specific moment in your life when you found peace and strength through prayer during a financial challenge. Reflect on how your faith and prayer helped you overcome stress. Write down your thoughts in your journal.

_____
_____
_____
_____
_____
_____
_____
_____
_____
_____
_____
_____
_____
_____
_____
_____

Life Application: Today, make a commitment to turn to prayer and wise financial management to overcome financial stress. Seek God's guidance in your financial matters and, where needed, reach out to financial advisors or mentors for support.

How can you apply this in your life?

_____
_____
_____
_____
_____
_____

Closing Prayer
Heavenly Father, grant me peace and guidance to overcome financial stress. May I find strength in prayer, making wise decisions for peace and stability. Trusting Your peace to guard my heart and mind as I navigate financial challenges.
In Jesus' name, I pray.
Amen.

Practical Solution for a Financial Need

Virtual Bible Trivia Nights

Host virtual Bible trivia events where participants can compete individually or in teams. Charge an entry fee and offer prizes for winners. This can be a fun and engaging way for people to test their knowledge of Scripture.

Week 28: Gratitude for Financial Breakthroughs

Date:

Bible Reading: Psalm 100:4-5
Enter into His gates with thanksgiving, and into His courts with praise. Be thankful to Him, and bless His name. For the LORD is good; His mercy is everlasting, and His truth endures to all generations.

Devotional:
Gratitude is a powerful practice that deepens our connection with God. Psalm 100:4-5 reminds us to enter God's presence with thanksgiving and praise, acknowledging His goodness, love, and faithfulness. When we experience financial breakthroughs, it's essential to express gratitude for the blessings we've received.

Reflection:
Gratitude is a transformative force, honoring God and reshaping our perspective on financial success. It redirects our attention from scarcity to abundance, acknowledging that all we possess is a divine gift. By expressing gratitude for financial breakthroughs, we affirm that our faith rests in God's ongoing provision, fostering a strengthened reliance on Him. This shift in mindset underscores the role of gratitude in recognizing the origin of our blessings and reinforces the importance of continually looking to God as the ultimate provider in our financial journey. It's a practical acknowledgment that gratitude is not just a sentiment but a catalyst for enduring faith and reliance on divine provision.

Daily Prayer
Heavenly Father, instill in me a heart of generosity and compassion toward those in need.
Help me share Your blessings with others and be a conduit of Your love. May I be mindful of opportunities to bless others abundantly.
In Jesus' name, I pray.
Amen.

What is your takeaway from these scriptures?

Journaling Prompt: Take a moment to reflect on recent financial breakthroughs you've experienced. Consider the emotions and thoughts that arose during these moments. Write down your reflections in your journal.

_____
_____
_____
_____
_____
_____
_____
_____
_____
_____
_____
_____
_____
_____
_____
_____
_____
_____
_____
_____

Life Application: Today, make a commitment to cultivate a heart of gratitude for your financial blessings. Take time to thank God for the financial breakthroughs you've experienced and for His ongoing provision in your life. Express your gratitude in your daily life through prayer and actions.

How can you apply this in your life?

_____
_____
_____
_____
_____

Closing Prayer
Heavenly Father,
I express gratitude for financial breakthroughs. Thank You for provision and faithfulness. Grant me grace to maintain a grateful heart on this financial journey, recognizing that all good things come from You.
In Jesus' name, I pray.
Amen.

_____
_____
_____
_____
_____
_____
_____
_____

Practical Solution for a Financial Need

Faith-Based Subscription Box

Curate and sell subscription boxes filled with faith-inspired items such as books, devotionals, art, and handmade goods. Subscribers receive a monthly package of encouragement.

Week 29: Financial Patience and God's Timing

Date:

Bible Reading: Ecclesiastes 3:1
To everything there is a season, a time for every purpose under heaven.

Devotional: Ecclesiastes 3:1 reminds us that there is a time for every activity under the heavens. This principle applies to our financial journey, highlighting the importance of patience and trusting in God's perfect timing.

Reflection:
Financial decision-making requires patience, recognizing God's sovereign timing intricately woven into the fabric of our lives. This wisdom urges trust in divine orchestration, appreciating that waiting on God's timing yields rich blessings. In patient moments, we deepen reliance on His guidance, permitting His timing to unfold. This cultivation of patience fosters a profound connection with His wisdom, illuminating the path to financial prosperity. It's an acknowledgment that the journey involves more than immediate outcomes, underscoring the importance of aligning with divine timing as we navigate financial decisions. The quiet perseverance allows us to witness the unfolding of God's plan, guiding us towards enduring financial wisdom and prosperity.

Daily Prayer
Heavenly Father, teach me contentment in all circumstances, whether in abundance or lack. Help me find satisfaction in You alone and not in material possessions. May my joy come from knowing You and walking in Your ways. In Jesus' name, I pray. Amen.

What is your takeaway from this scripture?

Journaling Prompts: Reflect on your current perspective on timing in your financial journey. How can Ecclesiastes 3:1 shape your approach to patience?

Consider moments in your life when God's timing proved to be perfect. How did these experiences deepen your trust in His guidance?

In what areas of your financial life do you need to exercise patience? How can you actively trust in God's timing in these specific areas?

_____
_____
_____
_____
_____
_____
_____
_____
_____
_____
_____
_____
_____
_____
_____
_____
_____

Life Application: Think about practical ways to cultivate patience in your financial decisions. This might involve setting realistic expectations, waiting on God's guidance, and trusting that His timing is perfect.

How can you apply this in your life?

_____
_____
_____
_____
_____
_____

Closing Prayer

Heavenly Father,
help me trust Your perfect plan for my finances. I surrender worries to You and seek Your guidance. As I align my financial journey with Your plan, may prosperity, hope, and a promising future unfold.
In Jesus' name, I pray.
Amen.

Practical Solution for a Financial Need

Faith-Based Social Media Consulting

Offer consulting services to churches, ministries, or individuals looking to enhance their online presence. Provide guidance on social media strategy, content creation, and community engagement from a Christian perspective.

Week 30: A Life Transformed

Date:

Bible Reading: Romans 12:2
I beseech you therefore, brethren, by the mercies of God, that you present your bodies a living sacrifice, holy, acceptable to God, which is your reasonable service.

Devotional:
A transformed life is the culmination of your journey towards financial breakthrough. Romans 12:2 encourages us not to conform to the world's patterns but to be transformed through the renewing of our minds. This transformation is a continuous process that involves aligning your financial decisions, values, and desires with God's will.

Reflection:
Romans 12:2 advises against adopting the world's mindset, urging a transformative renewal of the mind. It emphasizes breaking free from societal norms, allowing God's perspective to shape our thoughts. This renewal facilitates discernment to understand and align with God's will, distinguishing what is good, pleasing, and perfect in His eyes. The call to nonconformity underscores the challenge of resisting cultural pressures and prevailing values, promoting a counter-cultural mindset. The passage serves as a guide for believers, encouraging them to resist conformity, actively engage in mind renewal, and discern God's will for a life characterized by goodness, pleasing actions, and alignment with His perfect plan.

Daily Prayer
Heavenly Father, grant me discernment in distinguishing between worldly success and Kingdom priorities. Help me align my ambitions with Your purposes and seek first Your kingdom above all else. May my pursuits bring glory to Your name.
In Jesus' name, I pray.
Amen.

What is your takeaway from this scripture?

Journaling Prompts: Take time to reflect on the transformation you've experienced in your financial journey throughout this prayer journal. Consider the insights, growth, and changes that have occurred. Write down your reflections in your journal.

_____
_____
_____
_____
_____
_____
_____
_____
_____
_____
_____
_____
_____
_____
_____
_____
_____

Life Application: As you complete this prayer journal, make a commitment to continue seeking transformation in your financial journey and aligning your choices with God's will. Trust that the work God has begun in you will lead to a life that glorifies Him in all areas, including your finances.

How can you apply this in your life?

_____
_____
_____
_____
_____
_____

Closing Prayer
Heavenly Father,
I'm grateful for the transformation in my financial journey. Guide and strengthen me to seek Your perfect will in decisions. May my life testify to Your goodness and grace.
In Jesus' name, I pray.
Amen.

Practical Solution for a Financial Need

Christian Podcast Production Services

Offer podcast production services with a Christian focus. Assist individuals or ministries in launching and managing their own podcasts, handling tasks like editing, scripting, and distribution.

Week 31: The Blessing of Generosity

Date:

Bible Reading: Proverbs 11:25
The generous soul will be made rich, and he who waters will also be watered himself.

Devotional:
Proverbs 11:25 beautifully shows us that when we give generously, we not only experience blessings and refreshment, but our open-hearted generosity becomes a source of joy and blessing for others as well. It's a wonderful reminder that sharing kindness and goodness creates a positive and uplifting cycle for everyone involved.

Reflection:
Embracing generosity as a cornerstone in your journey toward financial breakthrough involves more than just the act of giving money. It's about cultivating a heartfelt and open-handed spirit that extends its influence into every nook and cranny of your life. This generosity goes beyond the tangible currency and finds expression in kindness, time, and compassion. Whether it's a warm smile, a lending hand, or a thoughtful gesture, infusing generosity into your daily interactions creates a ripple effect that can bring joy not only to others but also back into your own life, fostering a sense of abundance and community. So, as you embark on your financial breakthrough journey, consider generosity as a multi-faceted jewel that can illuminate and enrich every step of the way.

Daily Prayer

Heavenly Father, grant me wisdom to honor You with my financial decisions. Help me discern between needs and wants, and guide me in stewarding Your resources faithfully. May Your grace lead me on the path to financial freedom and abundance. In Jesus' name, I pray. Amen.

What is your takeaway from this scripture?

Journaling Prompts: Reflect on your current perspective on generosity. In what ways can you deepen your commitment to a generous lifestyle?

Consider the connection between generosity and prosperity. How have you experienced the reciprocal blessings of giving? What practical steps can you take to be more generous in your finances? How can you actively refresh others through your generosity?

_____
_____
_____
_____
_____
_____
_____
_____
_____
_____
_____
_____
_____
_____
_____
_____

Life Application Reflection: Think about concrete ways to incorporate generosity into your financial practices. This might involve regular charitable giving, supporting local initiatives, and finding opportunities to bless others with your resources.

How can you apply this in your life?

_____
_____
_____
_____
_____
_____

Closing Prayer
Heavenly Father, cultivate in me a generous heart. Teach me to refresh others with the resources You've entrusted to me. May my acts of generosity lead to prosperity, and may I be a conduit of Your blessings to those around me.
In Jesus' name, I pray.
Amen.

Practical Solution for a Financial Need

Virtual Christian Mentorship Programs

Establish virtual mentorship programs where you provide one-on-one guidance and support to individuals seeking spiritual or professional development.
Charge a reasonable fee for your mentorship services.

Week 32: Finding Contentment in God's Provision

Date:

Bible Reading: Hebrews 13:5
Let your conduct be without covetousness; be content with such things as you have. For He Himself has said, "I will never leave you nor forsake you."

Devotional:
Hebrews 13:5 lovingly reminds us to delve into the profound well of contentment that resides within the vast expanse of God's generous provision. This verse serves as a gentle reminder that His constant presence stands as an enduring reservoir of fulfillment, far surpassing the fleeting and transient satisfaction that often accompanies the pursuit of material wealth.

Reflection:
At the heart of the journey toward financial breakthrough lies the foundational element of contentment. It's not merely the absence of financial strife but a deep recognition of God's unwavering faithfulness. This understanding compels us to embrace a state of heart and mind that comprehends His enduring commitment. It's the assurance that even amid the unpredictable ebb and flow of financial circumstances, God remains our steadfast companion, offering a tranquility that outshines the alluring but ephemeral glow of amassed riches.

Daily Prayer
Heavenly Father, bless my efforts to cultivate a spirit of discipline in managing finances. Help me resist impulse spending and embrace frugality. May I be diligent in budgeting and saving, trusting You to provide for my needs.
In Jesus' name, I pray.
Amen.

What is your takeaway from this scripture?

Journaling Prompt: Reflect on a financial decision you need to make. How can you align it with God's kingdom principles, considering His righteousness?

_____
_____
_____
_____
_____
_____
_____
_____
_____
_____
_____
_____
_____
_____
_____
_____
_____
_____
_____

Life Application Reflection: Think about practical steps you can take to shift your financial priorities to align with God's kingdom. This might involve adjusting your budget, reconsidering spending habits, or redirecting financial resources towards Kingdom-focused activities.

How can you apply this in your life?

_____
_____
_____
_____
_____
_____

Closing Prayer

Heavenly Father,
guide me in seeking Your kingdom first in all aspects of my financial life. Help me prioritize Your will over my desires. May my financial decisions be rooted in righteousness and bring glory to Your name.
In Jesus' name, I pray.
Amen.

Practical Solution for a Financial Need

Faith-Based Gardening Workshops

Combine the love of gardening with faith by organizing workshops on cultivating a garden with Biblical plants or themes. Offer these workshops online or in person, charging a membership fee for participation.

Week 33: Faithfulness in Tithing

Date:

Bible Reading: 2 Corinthians 4:18
While we do not look at the things which are seen, but at the things which are not seen. For the things which are seen are temporary, but the things which are not seen are eternal.

Devotional:
Guided by 2 Corinthians 4:18, we're prompted to direct our gaze toward the eternal, acknowledging that financial challenges are but fleeting. This verse invites us to face difficulties with faith, fully trusting in the enduring promises of God. By adopting an eternal perspective, we find the strength to navigate temporary financial struggles, understanding that they are overshadowed by the unwavering assurance of God's lasting and transformative promises for our lives.

Reflection:
Amid financial challenges, faith becomes a steadfast anchor, steadying our journey. This unwavering belief surpasses immediate struggles, prompting us to focus on God's eternal perspective. In times of financial uncertainty, faith calls for trust in His unchanging character and unwavering promises. It serves as a resilient assurance, urging us to look beyond the hardships, grounded in the steadfast belief that God's enduring nature and reliable promises transcend temporary financial difficulties, providing solace and direction in navigating uncertain moments.

Daily Prayer
Heavenly Father, grant me courage to face financial challenges with faith and resilience. Help me trust Your faithfulness in times of scarcity and uncertainty. May I find strength in Your promises and persevere with hope. In Jesus' name, I pray. Amen.

What is your takeaway from this scripture?

Journaling Prompts: Reflect on your current views on tithing. How do you perceive the act of giving a tenth of your income back to God?

Recall instances where you've experienced God's faithfulness in your financial life, particularly through tithing. In what ways can you deepen your commitment to tithing? Consider your current practices and how you can align them more closely with God's principles.

_____
_____
_____
_____
_____
_____
_____
_____
_____
_____
_____
_____
_____
_____
_____
_____
_____

Life Application Reflection: Think about practical steps you can take to honor God through your tithing. Consider creating a budget that includes tithing as a priority, and reflect on the impact of your obedience on your financial outlook.

How can you apply this in your life?

_____
_____
_____
_____
_____
_____
_____
_____
_____
_____
_____
_____
_____

Closing Prayer

Heavenly Father,
I declare my trust in Your provision for all my financial needs this week. Lord, I surrender my financial concerns to You. Help me trust in Your promises of provision and blessings as I honor You with my finances. Grant me the faithfulness to tithe with a cheerful heart, knowing that You are faithful to pour out blessings beyond measure.
In Jesus' name, I pray.
Amen.

Practical Solution for a Financial Need

Christian Virtual Assistant Services

Provide virtual assistant services specifically for Christian entrepreneurs, ministries, or organizations. Offer administrative support, social media management, and other tasks aligned with faith-based values.

Week 34: God's Economy of Abundant Blessings

Date:

Bible Reading: Acts 20:35
"I have shown you in every way, by laboring like this, that you must support the weak. And remember the words of the Lord Jesus, that He said, 'It is more blessed to give than to receive.'"

Devotional:
In Acts 20:35, an echo of Jesus' teachings emphasizes the reciprocal joy of giving and receiving. This powerful reminder underscores that generosity is a profound source of blessing, not just for those who receive but equally for those who give. It encapsulates the transformative nature of a generous spirit, highlighting the mutual joy that arises when you engage in acts of kindness, fostering a cycle of blessings that enrich both the giver and the receiver.

Reflection:
The joy inherent in both giving and receiving is intricately woven into the fabric of generosity. This principle serves as a poignant reminder that, as we willingly open our hearts to engage in the dual acts of giving and receiving, we actively participate in God's economy of abundant blessings. It's a beautiful testament to the interconnectedness of joy, generosity, and the divine reciprocity that enriches the lives of both the giver and the receiver in profound and meaningful ways.

Daily Prayer
Heavenly Father, guide me in aligning my financial goals with Your kingdom purposes. Help me invest my time, talents, and resources in endeavors that honor You. May my life be a testimony of Your goodness and provision. In Jesus' name, I pray. Amen.

What is your takeaway from this scripture?

Journaling Prompts: Reflect on moments when you've experienced joy through giving. How does generosity contribute to your sense of fulfillment?

In what ways can you actively balance both giving and receiving in your financial life? How might this balance contribute to a greater sense of joy?

_____
_____
_____
_____
_____
_____
_____
_____
_____
_____
_____
_____
_____
_____
_____
_____
_____

Life Application Reflection: Think about practical ways you can incorporate the joy of giving and receiving into your financial practices. This might involve intentional acts of kindness, being open to receiving help when needed, and expressing gratitude for both.

How can you apply this in your life?

_____
_____
_____
_____
_____
_____
_____
_____
_____
_____
_____
_____
_____

> **Closing Prayer**
> Heavenly Father, help me maintain an attitude of gratitude as I trust in Your financial blessings. Lord Jesus, teach me the joy found in both giving and receiving. May my generosity be a source of blessing to others, and may I be open to receiving the blessings You provide through the kindness of others. Help me to balance both with a grateful heart. In Jesus' name, I pray. Amen.

Practical Solution for a Financial Need

Christian Interior Design Consulting

Offer interior design services with a Christian touch. Help individuals create spaces that reflect their faith through decor, colors, and design elements. Charge for your consulting and design services.

Week 35: The Blessing of Openhanded Generosity

Date:

Bible Reading: Deuteronomy 15:10-11
"You shall surely give to him, and your heart should not be grieved when you give to him, because for this thing the LORD your God will bless you in all your works and in all to which you put your hand. "For the poor will never cease from the land; therefore I command you, saying, 'You shall open your hand wide to your brother, to your poor and your needy, in your land.'

Devotional:
Deuteronomy 15:10-11 implores us to embrace generous giving with a cheerful heart, assuring that God will bless the fruits of our labor in return. This passage underscores the profound blessing that emanates from openhanded generosity toward those in need. It's a call to engage in acts of kindness with genuine joy, acknowledging that God not only honors our generosity but magnifies the impact of our open hearts, fostering a cycle of blessings that transcends our initial act of giving.

Reflection:
Deuteronomy 15:10-11 encourages a shift towards openhanded generosity, highlighting the transformative impact such generosity can have, not only on the recipient but also on the giver. This timeless wisdom invites us to reconsider our perspective on giving, recognizing it as a source of blessings that reverberate throughout the entire act of generosity, enriching the lives of all involved.

Daily Prayer

Heavenly Father, grant me discernment in seeking financial opportunities. Help me recognize blessings disguised as challenges and embrace them with faith. May I step out in courage and seize the divine appointments You have prepared for me.
In Jesus' name, I pray.
Amen.

What is your takeaway from these scriptures?

Journaling Prompts: Reflect on your current attitude toward giving. How might Deuteronomy 15:10-11 encourage you to cultivate a more openhanded and generous spirit?

Consider the promise of blessing associated with openhanded generosity. How have you experienced blessings in your life as a result of giving generously? How can you actively cultivate a generous spirit without a grudging heart?

_____
_____
_____
_____
_____
_____
_____
_____
_____
_____
_____
_____
_____
_____
_____
_____
_____

Life Application Reflection: Think about practical ways to incorporate intentional prayer, petition, and gratitude into your financial life. Establishing a routine of bringing your financial concerns to God and expressing gratitude for His provision can be transformative.

How can you apply this in your life?

_____
_____
_____
_____
_____
_____

Closing Prayer

Heavenly Father,
I place my financial goals in Your hands, trusting in Your divine guidance.
I bring my financial worries before You. Grant me Your peace that surpasses all understanding. Help me to trust in Your perfect plan, presenting my concerns to You with gratitude and faith.
Guard my heart and mind.
In Jesus' name, I pray.
Amen.

_____
_____
_____
_____
_____
_____

Practical Solution for a Financial Need

Virtual Christian Art Workshops for Kids

Host virtual art workshops for children with a Christian theme.
Teach kids to express their faith through creative projects.
Parents can pay for their children to participate
in these engaging and educational sessions.

Week 36: Faithfulness in Financial Planning

Date:

Bible Reading: Proverbs 16:9
A man's heart plans his way, but the LORD directs his steps.

Devotional:
Proverbs 16:9 illustrates the collaborative nature of our planning with God's divine guidance. This wisdom recognizes that although we engage in human planning, the ultimate direction of our steps lies in the hands of the Lord. It underscores the symbiotic relationship between our efforts and God's sovereignty, urging us to approach our plans with humility and a profound trust in His overarching guidance that establishes and directs the course of our journey.

Reflection:
Within the context of financial planning, Proverbs 16:9 serves as a poignant reminder to surrender our plans to God. It underscores the imperative of acknowledging His sovereignty in every aspect of our financial journey. This verse prompts us to approach our financial decisions with a spirit of submission, recognizing that the Lord's divine guidance shapes and directs our plans. It encourages a posture of humility, inviting us to trust in His overarching wisdom for a prosperous financial path.

Daily Prayer
Heavenly Father, bless my family with unity and wisdom in financial matters. Help us communicate openly and make decisions together. May Your peace reign in our home as we seek Your guidance and provision.
In Jesus' name, I pray.
Amen.

What is your takeaway from this scripture?

Journaling Prompt: Reflect on your current approach to financial planning. How might Proverbs 16:9 influence your mindset as you make plans for your financial future? Consider the idea of submitting your financial plans to the Lord. In what ways can you actively seek His guidance in your financial decision-making?

_____
_____
_____
_____
_____
_____
_____
_____
_____
_____
_____
_____
_____
_____
_____
_____
_____
_____
_____

Life Application Reflection: Think about practical ways to integrate God's guidance into your financial planning. This might involve setting aside dedicated time for prayer and reflection before making financial decisions, and being open to adjustments based on God's leading.

How can you apply this in your life?

_____
_____
_____
_____
_____
_____
_____
_____
_____
_____
_____
_____
_____
_____
_____
_____

Closing Prayer

Heavenly Father,
I trust in Your promises for financial abundance and prosperity. I submit my financial plans to You, acknowledging Your sovereignty. Establish my steps according to Your will. Guide me in every decision, and may my financial planning be aligned with Your purpose for my life. Grant me the wisdom to discern Your leading in all aspects of my financial journey.
In Jesus' name, I pray.
Amen.

Practical Solution for a Financial Need

Christian Freelance Photography

Provide freelance photography services with a focus on capturing special moments for Christian events or family gatherings. Offer packages that include professional photo sessions and prints.

Week 37: God's Boundless Grace and Provision

Bible Reading: 2 Corinthians 9:8
And God is able to make all grace abound toward you, that you, always having all sufficiency in all things, may have an abundance for every good work.

Devotional:
2 Corinthians 9:8 directs our focus to God's capacity to abundantly bless us. Today, let's contemplate the profound connection between His abundance and the contentment it brings, especially within the context of our finances. This verse encourages us to explore the harmonious interplay between God's generous blessings and the deep-seated contentment that arises when we align our lives, including our financial endeavors, with His gracious and abundant provision.

Reflection:
The richness of God's blessings envelopes every facet of our existence. Genuine contentment, according to 2 Corinthians 9:8, lies not in the accumulation of possessions but in the profound acknowledgment of God's boundless grace and provision. This wisdom encourages a shift in perspective, guiding us to find true satisfaction in the limitless abundance of God's blessings that go beyond the tangible and permeate the entirety of our lives.

Daily Prayer
Heavenly Father, guard my heart against the love of money and material possessions. Help me find true fulfillment in You alone. May I lay up treasures in heaven and invest in eternal rewards.
In Jesus' name, I pray.
Amen.

What is your takeaway from this scripture?

Journaling Prompts: What does contentment mean to you in the context of your financial journey? How has your definition evolved over time?

Reflect on moments when you've experienced God's abundant blessings. How did these moments influence your sense of contentment?

In what ways can you cultivate contentment in all areas of your life, including your finances?

What practices or perspectives might help you achieve this?

_____
_____
_____
_____
_____
_____
_____
_____
_____
_____
_____
_____
_____
_____

Life Application Reflection: Consider practical steps to cultivate contentment in your financial life. This might involve simplifying your lifestyle, expressing gratitude for what you have, and intentionally focusing on the non-material aspects of abundance.

How can you apply this in your life?

_____
_____
_____
_____
_____
_____

Closing Prayer

Heavenly Father, thank You for Your abundant blessings. As I navigate my financial journey, teach me the true meaning of contentment. May my heart be grateful for Your provision in all things, and may I find joy in Your abundant grace.
In Jesus' name, I pray.
Amen.

Practical Solution for a Financial Need

Virtual Christian Language Exchange

Facilitate language exchange programs with a Christian twist.
Connect individuals wanting to learn a new language
while integrating Bible study or Christian teachings
into the language learning process.
Charge a membership fee for participation.

Week 38: Embracing Financial Discipline

Date:

Bible Reading: Proverbs 21:20
There is desirable treasure, and oil in the dwelling of the wise, but a foolish man squanders it.

Devotional:
The imagery of storing up choice food and olive oil speaks to the intentional, thoughtful approach to managing resources that leads to abundance.

Reflection:
This scripture encourages reflection on the wisdom of thoughtful and intentional living. The metaphor of storing up choice food and olive oil implies a deliberate and prudent approach to life's provisions. It suggests the importance of making wise choices, investing in quality, and preparing for the future. Conversely, the image of fools who hastily consume their resources without consideration highlights the contrast of impulsive and shortsighted behavior. The scripture prompts contemplation on the value of foresight, responsible stewardship, and the long-term benefits that come from making deliberate choices in various aspects of life. It serves as a timeless reminder to approach life with wisdom and discernment, seeking to cultivate and store up that which is truly valuable.

Daily Prayer
Heavenly Father, grant me creativity in generating multiple streams of income. Help me explore new opportunities and maximize my potential. May I use my talents and resources to glorify You and bless others.
In Jesus' name, I pray.
Amen.

What is your takeaway from this scripture?

Journaling Prompts: Reflect on your current financial habits. In what areas of your life can you exercise more discipline?

Consider a time when financial discipline positively impacted your life. How did this experience shape your understanding of wise financial choices? What practical steps can you take to cultivate financial discipline in your daily life? Think about both short-term and long-term goals.

_____
_____
_____
_____
_____
_____
_____
_____
_____
_____
_____
_____
_____
_____
_____

Life Application Reflection: Think about tangible ways you can implement financial discipline in your life. This might involve setting savings goals, or identifying areas where spending can be more intentional.

How can you apply this in your life?

_____
_____
_____
_____
_____
_____
_____
_____
_____
_____
_____
_____
_____

Closing Prayer

Heavenly Father, grant me the wisdom to be disciplined in my financial choices. Help me make intentional decisions that align with Your plans for my prosperity. May my actions reflect Your guidance, leading to a life of abundance and wise stewardship.
In Jesus' name, I pray.
Amen.

Practical Solution for a Financial Need

Faith-Based Mobile Apps Development

Develop mobile apps that cater to the spiritual needs of users. This could include prayer apps, devotionals, or interactive Bible study apps. Monetize through app purchases or subscriptions.

Week 39: Seeking God's Guidance in Financial Decisions

Date:

Bible Reading: Proverbs 3:5-6
Trust in the LORD with all your heart, and lean not on your own understanding; In all your ways acknowledge Him and He shall direct your paths.

Devotional:
In the realm of finances, the call to trust God carries profound implications. It beckons us to surrender not just a portion, but every facet of our financial lives to His sovereign control. Trusting God in financial matters involves a deliberate shift in our mindset, recognizing His wisdom as superior to our own limited understanding.

Reflection:
Entrusting God with our finances involves recognizing Him as the ultimate source of wisdom in stewardship, budgeting, investments, and every financial decision. It's more than acknowledgment; it's a deliberate surrender, a conscious act of placing trust in His omniscient hands. This intentional reliance on God's guidance underscores a conscious decision to seek His wisdom and submit to His authority in financial matters. It is an act of acknowledging our limitations and recognizing God's infinite understanding, inviting His discernment into our financial decisions. Trusting God with our finances signifies an intentional and purposeful surrender of control, aligning our actions with the recognition of His supreme wisdom.

Daily Prayer
Heavenly Father,
fill me with gratitude for Your provision and faithfulness.
Help me cultivate a thankful heart in every season of life.
May I never lose sight of Your abundant blessings and grace.
In Jesus' name, I pray.
Amen.

What is your takeaway from these scriptures?

Journaling Prompts: Consider instances in your financial journey where you've experienced moments of surrender to God's guidance.

How did these moments influence the outcomes of your decisions?

Reflect on the areas of your financial life where uncertainties exist. How can an intentional trust in God's guidance bring peace and assurance in the face of the unknown?

_____
_____
_____
_____
_____
_____
_____
_____
_____
_____
_____
_____
_____
_____
_____
_____
_____

Life Application Reflection: Think about practical ways you can actively surrender your financial decisions to God. This might involve incorporating prayer into your budgeting process, seeking biblical financial advice, and aligning your financial goals with God's principles.

How can you apply this in your life?

_____
_____
_____
_____
_____
_____
_____
_____
_____
_____
_____
_____
_____
_____
_____

Closing Prayer

Heavenly Father, guide me to opportunities that align with Your plan for my financial success. I surrender every aspect of my financial life to You. In the realm of finances, where uncertainties often prevail, I choose to trust Your wisdom over my own understanding. Guide me in every decision, big or small, and may my financial choices be a reflection of my complete reliance on Your unfailing guidance.
In Jesus' name, I pray.
Amen.

Practical Solution for a Financial Need

Christian Virtual Choir or Music Group

Organize and lead a virtual choir or music group with a Christian repertoire. Performances can be shared through virtual concerts or events.

Week 40: Finding Financial Freedom

Date:

Bible Reading: Luke 14:28-30
"For which of you, intending to build a tower, does not sit down first and count the cost, whether he has enough to finish it—"lest, after he has laid the foundation, and is not able to finish, all who see it begin to mock him, "saying, 'This man began to build and was not able to finish.'

Devotional:
In Luke 14:28-30, Jesus uses the metaphor of building a tower to emphasize the importance of careful planning and financial discipline. It underscores the value of counting the cost before embarking on any financial endeavor.

Reflection:
The analogy of building a tower underscores the significance of evaluating the costs and commitments before embarking on a project. It encourages thoughtful consideration and preparation to ensure successful completion. Just as a builder wouldn't commence construction without assessing available resources, you are urged to approach their goals with a realistic understanding of the challenges ahead. Beyond financial implications, the passage speaks to the broader theme of commitment and perseverance. By diligently estimating the costs before initiating a venture, one not only avoids potential setbacks but also cultivates a reputation for reliability and diligence.

Daily Prayer
Heavenly Father, surround me with wise counselors who will speak truth and encouragement into my financial journey. Help me heed their advice and learn from their experiences.
May I grow in wisdom and discernment as I walk in Your ways.
In Jesus' name, I pray.
Amen.

What is your takeaway from these scriptures?

Journaling Prompts: Consider your current financial goals as a "tower" you're building. What steps have you taken to estimate the cost and ensure completion?

Reflect on the potential consequences of not carefully planning your financial endeavors. How can discipline prevent ridicule in your financial journey?

_____
_____
_____
_____
_____
_____
_____
_____
_____
_____
_____
_____
_____
_____
_____
_____

Life Application Reflection: Think about practical steps you can take to enhance your financial discipline. This might involve setting realistic financial goals, or seeking advice from financial experts.

How can you apply this in your life?

_____
_____
_____
_____
_____
_____
_____
_____
_____
_____
_____
_____
_____

Closing Prayer

Heavenly Father,
I trust in Your ability to lead me to financial prosperity this week. Grant me the discipline and wisdom to carefully plan my financial endeavors. Help me count the cost before embarking on any financial journey and guide me in building a strong foundation for financial freedom. May my actions be a testament to Your wisdom. In Jesus' name, I pray.
Amen.

Practical Solution for a Financial Need

Christian Art and Crafts

Create and sell artwork, crafts, or handmade items that reflect Christian themes. This could include paintings, jewelry, home decor, or custom items for special occasions.

Week 41: Understanding the Purpose of Wealth

Date:

Bible Reading: 1 Timothy 6:17-19
Command those who are rich in this present age not to be haughty, nor to trust in uncertain riches but in the living God, who gives us richly all things to enjoy. Let them do good, that they be rich in good works, ready to give, willing to share, storing up for themselves a good foundation for the time to come, that they may lay hold on eternal life.

Devotional:
Paul's words in 1 Timothy 6:17-19 provide a profound perspective on the purpose of wealth. It encourages us to see wealth not as an end in itself but as a means to participate in God's redemptive work.

Reflection:
Understanding wealth's purpose sparks a transformative shift, urging us beyond mere possession accumulation. It challenges us to perceive resources as tools for positive impact and stewardship, emphasizing a responsibility to contribute to the greater good and the realization of God's kingdom. It intertwines material wealth with a higher calling, encouraging intentional and purposeful use of resources to contribute positively to the world, aligning actions with a broader vision of stewardship and impact.

Daily Prayer
Heavenly Father, grant me resilience in times of financial hardship. Help me trust Your provision and seek Your guidance with unwavering faith. May Your strength sustain me through every trial, leading me to greater dependence on Your grace. In Jesus' name, I pray. Amen.

What is your takeaway from these scriptures?

Journaling Prompts: Reflect on your current perspective on wealth. In what ways can you align it more closely with Paul's teachings in 1 Timothy?

Consider the uncertainty of wealth. How can you shift your hope from material possessions to God, who richly provides for our enjoyment?

How can you actively be rich in good deeds and generous in sharing your resources with others? Consider specific actions you can take.

Life Application Reflection: Think about practical ways you can use your wealth for the betterment of others and for the advancement of God's kingdom. This might involve charitable giving, volunteering, or investing in initiatives that align with your values.

How can you apply this in your life?

_____
_____
_____
_____
_____
_____
_____
_____
_____
_____
_____
_____
_____

Closing Prayer

Heavenly Father,
I place my financial endeavors in Your hands, trusting in Your divine plan. Help me understand the true purpose of wealth. May I not place my hope in uncertain riches but in You, who generously provides. Guide me in being rich in good deeds, generous, and willing to share, so that my life may truly reflect
Your purpose.
In Jesus' name, I pray.
Amen.

Practical Solution for a Financial Need

Custom Scripture Art and Calligraphy

Create custom calligraphy pieces or artwork featuring favorite Bible verses or personalized messages. Sell these items online or at local craft fairs.

Week 42: Financial Alignment and Purpose

Date:

Bible Reading: Matthew 6:24

"No one can serve two masters; for either he will hate the one and love the other, or else he will be loyal to the one and despise the other. You cannot serve God and mammon."

Devotional:

Matthew 6:24 imparts a profound truth regarding the potential conflict between serving God and serving money. This wisdom underscores the paramount importance of prioritizing stewardship over the relentless pursuit of wealth. It challenges us to examine our allegiances, urging us to choose a path where our ultimate goal is to serve God through responsible stewardship, recognizing that our devotion to Him takes precedence over the fleeting allure of material riches.

Reflection:

Achieving financial freedom is intricately tied to our commitment to stewardship—a profound acknowledgment that our resources are entrusted to us by God. This commitment involves conscientiously managing our finances in alignment with His purposes. This perspective transforms our approach to finances, fostering a sense of purpose, responsibility, and gratitude.

Daily Prayer

Heavenly Father, bless me with a heart of generosity and compassion toward those in need. Help me extend Your love and grace to others through acts of kindness and generosity. May my life reflect Your abundant blessings and mercy. In Jesus' name, I pray. Amen.

What is your takeaway from this scripture?

Journaling Prompts: Reflect on your current approach to stewardship. In what ways can Matthew 6:24 guide you in prioritizing God over money?

Consider the balance between devotion to God and the pursuit of wealth. How can you actively ensure that your heart is devoted to God in your financial decisions?

Life Application Reflection: Think about practical ways to prioritize stewardship in your financial journey. This might involve revisiting your financial goals, evaluating spending habits, and seeking opportunities to use your resources for God's purposes.

How can you apply this in your life?

_____
_____
_____
_____
_____
_____

Closing Prayer

Heavenly Father,
I trust in Your ability to turn financial challenges into opportunities for growth. Help me to choose stewardship over the pursuit of wealth. May my heart be devoted to You in all aspects of my financial life. Guide me to use the resources You've entrusted to me for Your purposes, leading to true financial freedom.
In Jesus' name, I pray.
Amen.

Practical Solution for a Financial Need

Christian Wedding Vows Writing Service

Offer a service to help couples write personalized Christian wedding vows. Provide a unique and heartfelt touch to wedding ceremonies.

Week 43: Trusting God in Financial Challenges

Date:

Bible Reading: Psalm 34:8
Oh, taste and see that the LORD is good; blessed is the man who trusts in Him!

Devotional:
In times of financial challenges, Psalm 34:8 invites us to taste and see the goodness of the Lord. It encourages us to take refuge in Him, finding assurance that even in difficulties, God remains trustworthy.

Reflection:
Navigating financial challenges can be an overwhelming journey, marked by uncertainties and stress. However, amidst these trials, it is crucial to anchor ourselves in the unchanging goodness of God. Trusting Him in the midst of difficulties serves as a profound act of faith, providing a pathway to experience His unwavering faithfulness. In the face of economic uncertainties or hardships, turning to God becomes a source of strength and solace. It is in these moments of reliance that we often discover a refuge in His boundless love—a love that remains steadfast regardless of our circumstances. Embracing trust in God not only empowers us to endure financial challenges but also unveils a deeper understanding of His constant presence, offering comfort and hope along the way.

Daily Prayer
Heavenly Father, grant me wisdom to discern between the things I desire and the things I need in my financial decisions. Help me prioritize what truly matters and find contentment in Your provision. May my desires align with Your will and bring glory to Your name. In Jesus' name, I pray. Amen.

What is your takeaway from this scripture?

Journaling Prompts: Reflect on moments when you've tasted and seen God's goodness, especially during financial challenges. How did His faithfulness manifest?

Consider the concept of taking refuge in God in the context of your financial struggles. In what ways can you actively seek refuge in Him during difficult times?

_____
_____
_____
_____
_____
_____
_____
_____
_____
_____
_____
_____
_____
_____
_____
_____
_____
_____

Life Application Reflection: Think about practical ways to actively trust God in your financial challenges. This might involve seeking His guidance, maintaining a posture of gratitude, or finding refuge in prayer and meditation on His promises.

How can you apply this in your life?

_____
_____
_____
_____
_____
_____
_____
_____
_____
_____
_____
_____
_____
_____
_____

Closing Prayer

Heavenly Father,
I trust in Your grace to navigate financial challenges with faith and resilience. Heavenly Father, in times of financial challenges, I choose to trust in Your goodness and take refuge in Your unfailing love. Open my eyes to see Your provision and guide me through difficulties. May my trust in You be a testimony to Your faithfulness.
In Jesus' name, I pray.
Amen.

Practical Solution for a Financial Need

Christian Life Coaching for Entrepreneurs

Provide life coaching services tailored for Christian entrepreneurs. Help them align their business goals with their faith and values.

Week 44: The Joy of Faithfulness

Date:

Bible Reading: Matthew 25:21
"His lord said to him, 'Well done, good and faithful servant; you were faithful over a few things, I will make you ruler over many things. Enter into the joy of your lord.'

Devotional:
In Matthew 25:21, we find the parable of the faithful servant, highlighting the joy that comes from faithful financial stewardship. It's a reminder that our handling of resources, regardless of the amount, is significant to God.

Reflection:
Financial stewardship transcends mere money management; it embodies a holistic approach to aligning our actions with the divine purposes that God has set forth. It extends beyond the balance sheets and budgets, delving into the spiritual dimension of faithfully overseeing the resources entrusted to us. Embracing financial stewardship involves recognizing that our financial decisions have profound implications on our spiritual journey. It's about intentionally using our resources in ways that reflect God's values and contribute to His kingdom.

Daily Prayer
Heavenly Father, bless me with a spirit of diligence and excellence in my work. Help me honor You with my efforts and strive for excellence in all I do. May my labor be fruitful and bring glory to Your kingdom.
In Jesus' name, I pray.
Amen.

What is your takeaway from this scripture?

Journaling Prompts: Reflect on your role as a steward of the resources God has given you. How can you cultivate a mindset of faithful stewardship?

Consider areas of your financial life where you can demonstrate faithfulness with small things. How might these small acts contribute to a greater sense of stewardship?

_____
_____
_____
_____
_____
_____
_____
_____
_____
_____
_____
_____
_____
_____
_____
_____
_____
_____
_____

Life Application Reflection: Think about practical ways you can exercise faithful stewardship in your financial life. This might involve seeking opportunities to serve with your resources.

How can you apply this in your life?

_____
_____
_____
_____
_____
_____

Closing Prayer

Heavenly Father,
I surrender my financial goals to Your will, trusting in Your divine purpose. Lord, guide me in being a faithful steward of the resources You've entrusted to me. Help me find joy in the small acts of faithfulness and align my financial decisions with Your purposes. May my stewardship bring glory to Your name.
In Jesus' name, I pray.
Amen.

_____
_____
_____
_____
_____
_____
_____
_____
_____

Practical Solution for a Financial Need

Christian Wedding Photography

Specialize in Christian wedding photography, capturing the sacred moments of couples who desire a photographer with a faith-focused approach. Offer packages that include pre-wedding prayer sessions or devotionals.

Week 45: Investing in Eternal Treasures

Date:

Bible Reading: Matthew 6:19-21
"Do not lay up for yourselves treasures on earth, where moth and rust destroy and where thieves break in and steal; but lay up for yourselves treasures in heaven, where neither moth nor rust destroys and where thieves do not break in and steal. For where your treasure is, there your heart will be also."

Devotional:
In Matthew 6:19-21, Jesus urges us to shift our focus from earthly treasures to eternal ones. It's a call to invest our resources in things that have lasting value, transcending the temporary nature of material wealth.

Reflection:
Engaging in the pursuit of eternal treasures beckons us to transcend the temporal perspective of financial decisions. It calls for a profound contemplation of the far-reaching implications of our choices, not just within the confines of the present moment but within the expansive framework of God's eternal kingdom. This transformative outlook prompts us to view wealth not solely as a means for immediate gratification or personal gain but as a tool to contribute to something enduring and divine. In the pursuit of eternal treasures, financial decisions are infused with a sense of purpose that extends beyond our immediate circumstances, compelling us to consider how our stewardship aligns with God's eternal plan.

Daily Prayer
Heavenly Father, guide me in setting financial goals that reflect Your priorities for my life. Help me be intentional in stewarding my resources and aligning my ambitions with Your kingdom purposes. May Your will be done in my finances. In Jesus' name, I pray. Amen.

What is your takeaway from these scriptures?

Journaling Prompts: Reflect on your current investments, not just financially but in terms of time and energy. How aligned are they with eternal values?

Consider the things that occupy your heart and mind. In what ways can you adjust your priorities to align more closely with heavenly treasures?

_____
_____
_____
_____
_____
_____
_____
_____
_____
_____
_____
_____
_____
_____
_____
_____
_____
_____

Life Application Reflection: Think about practical ways you can shift your investments, both financial and non-financial, toward eternal treasures. This might involve intentional acts of kindness, supporting kingdom-focused initiatives, and prioritizing relationships and spiritual growth.

How can you apply this in your life?

_____
_____
_____
_____
_____
_____
_____
_____
_____
_____
_____
_____
_____
_____

Closing Prayer

Heavenly Father,
I declare my trust in Your unfailing provision for every area of my life. Help me recognize the temporary nature of earthly treasures and guide me in investing in things that have eternal value. May my heart be aligned with Your kingdom priorities, and may my investments reflect Your everlasting truths.
In Jesus' name, I pray.
Amen.

Practical Solution for a Financial Need

Virtual Christian Tutoring Services

Provide online tutoring services for subjects such as math, science, or language arts, integrating Christian principles into the learning experience.

Week 46: The Blessing of Financial Unity

Date:

Bible Reading: Ecclesiastes 4:9
Two are better than one, because they have a good reward for their labor.

Devotional:
Ecclesiastes 4:9 underscores the strength found in unity. This can apply to the realm of finances emphasizing the mutual support and encouragement that comes when individuals join together in financial matters.

Reflection:
Financial unity extends beyond pooling resources; it encapsulates the creation of a cohesive and supportive environment where you collectively thrive and navigate challenges with shared strength. It embodies a collaborative approach to financial well-being, emphasizing mutual support, understanding, and shared responsibility. In fostering this unity, a community emerges where the financial successes of one contribute to the prosperity of all, creating a resilient foundation for facing uncertainties. It transcends individual gain, promoting a shared vision that elevates the collective welfare. Financial unity is a powerful synergy, transforming financial endeavors into a collective journey marked by resilience, cooperation, and the shared pursuit of prosperity.

Daily Prayer
Heavenly Father, grant me peace in the midst of financial crisis. Help me trust in Your faithfulness and rely on Your word. May Your peace guard my heart and mind as I navigate trials and financial challenges.
In Jesus' name, I pray.
Amen.

What is your takeaway from this scripture?

Journaling Prompts: Reflect on your current approach to finances. In what ways can unity enhance your financial journey?

Consider the importance of mutual support in financial matters. How can you cultivate a spirit of teamwork with your family, friends, or community?

_____
_____
_____
_____
_____
_____
_____
_____
_____
_____
_____
_____
_____
_____
_____
_____
_____
_____

Life Application Reflection: Consider practical ways you can foster financial unity in your relationships. This might involve open communication about financial goals, collaborative budgeting, and seeking advice from trusted individuals.

How can you apply this in your life?

_____
_____
_____
_____
_____
_____
_____
_____
_____
_____
_____
_____
_____
_____

Closing Prayer

Heavenly Father,
I trust in Your wisdom to navigate financial challenges with grace and faith in my relationships. Lord, help me recognize the strength found in unity, especially in my financial journey. Guide me to cultivate a spirit of teamwork with those around me. May our shared efforts lead to a good return for our labor and create a supportive environment for financial growth.
In Jesus' name, I pray.
Amen.

Practical Solution for a Financial Need

Christian Graphic Design Templates

Create and sell customizable graphic design templates with Christian themes. These templates can be used for social media, presentations, or church events.

Week 47: Financial Integrity and Honesty

Date:

Bible Reading: Proverbs 10:9
He who walks with integrity walks securely, but he who perverts his ways will become known.

Devotional:
Proverbs 10:9 emphasizes the importance of financial integrity and honesty. It speaks to the security that comes from walking in integrity and the consequences of dishonesty.

Reflection:
Financial integrity extends beyond transactions; it reflects the core of our character. Securing financial matters requires a foundation of honesty, transparency, and unwavering commitment to ethical practices. This involves aligning financial decisions with a moral compass, ensuring actions echo principles of integrity. Upholding these values not only fosters a trustworthy financial environment but cultivates personal integrity resonating in broader life aspects. The commitment to financial integrity stands as a testament to one's character, shaping a reputation grounded in ethical conduct. This alignment of values extends far beyond the financial realm, contributing to a meaningful and principled life overall.

Daily Prayer
Heavenly Father, bless me with discernment in managing debt responsibly. Help me make wise decisions to reduce debt and live within my means. May I honor You with my financial choices and experience freedom from financial burdens.
In Jesus' name, I pray.
Amen.

What is your takeaway from this scripture?

Journaling Prompts: Reflect on your current approach to financial integrity. In what ways can you strengthen your commitment to honesty in financial matters?

Consider the sense of security that comes from financial integrity. How does knowing you walk in honesty impact your overall well-being?

Think about the potential consequences of dishonest financial practices. How can a commitment to integrity prevent these consequences?

_____
_____
_____
_____
_____
_____
_____
_____
_____
_____
_____
_____
_____
_____
_____
_____

Life Application Reflection: Think about practical ways you can enhance financial integrity in your life. This might involve reviewing your financial practices, being transparent in your dealings, and seeking accountability where honesty is crucial.

How can you apply this in your life?

_____
_____
_____
_____
_____
_____

Closing Prayer

Heavenly Father,
I declare my reliance on Your promises of abundance and provision in my life. Lord, guide me in walking with integrity in my financial matters. May my actions be rooted in honesty and transparency. Help me to navigate challenges with integrity, knowing that true security comes from walking in Your ways.
In Jesus' name, I pray.
Amen.

Practical Solution for a Financial Need

Christian Home Organization Services

Offer home organization and decluttering services with a Christian approach. Help individuals create peaceful and spiritually uplifting living spaces.

Week 48: Generational Blessings through Wise Finances

Date:

Bible Reading: Proverbs 13:22
A good man leaves an inheritance to his children's children, but the wealth of the sinner is stored up for the righteous.

Devotional:
Proverbs 13:22 provides insight into the impact of wise financial practices on future generations. It speaks to the legacy of those who prioritize stewardship, leaving a lasting inheritance for their descendants.

Reflection:
Making wise financial decisions today holds the power to create a ripple effect of blessings that surpasses our current circumstances, reaching and influencing generations to come. It involves acknowledging the far-reaching impact of our actions and understanding how they contribute to the lasting legacy we leave behind. By cultivating a mindset that prioritizes not only immediate gains but also the enduring well-being of future generations, we participate in the ongoing narrative of prosperity, wisdom, and foresight that shapes the legacy we bequeath to our descendants.

Daily Prayer
Heavenly Father, fill me with gratitude for Your abundant provision in my life. Help me cultivate a heart of thanksgiving and recognize Your blessings each day. May my life overflow with praise and gratitude to You. In Jesus' name, I pray. Amen.

What is your takeaway from this scripture?

Journaling Prompt: Reflect on the concept of leaving a financial legacy. What kind of legacy do you aspire to leave for your children and grandchildren?

Consider your current financial practices. In what ways can you align them with the idea of leaving a positive inheritance for future generations?

Reflect on any financial lessons you've learned from your ancestors. How can these lessons inform your approach to building a generational legacy?

_____
_____
_____
_____
_____
_____
_____
_____
_____
_____
_____
_____
_____
_____
_____
_____
_____

Life Application Reflection: Think about practical steps you can take to build a positive financial legacy. This might involve creating a will, implementing sound investment strategies, and imparting financial wisdom to the younger generation.

How can you apply this in your life?

_____
_____
_____
_____
_____
_____

Closing Prayer

Heavenly Father,
I come before You with a heart full of gratitude and trust. I acknowledge Your sovereignty over every aspect of my life, including the financial legacy I leave for my children. Lord, guide me in making wise financial decisions that align with Your will. Grant me the discernment to steward resources responsibly, with an eye toward leaving a meaningful inheritance for my children. May this legacy be not just material, but also one of faith, values, and love. I trust in Your provision and guidance, believing that as I seek Your will, You will ensure a lasting and impactful inheritance for generations to come.
In Jesus' name, I pray.
Amen.

Practical Solution for a Financial Need

Christian Interior Design Blog

Start a blog or YouTube channel focused on Christian interior design. Share tips, DIY projects, and inspirational content that combines faith with home decor.
Monetize through sponsored content and affiliate marketing.

Week 49: God's Provision and Strength

Date:

Bible Reading: Philippians 4:11-13
Not that I speak in regard to need, for I have learned in whatever state I am, to be content: I know how to be abased, and I know how to abound. Everywhere and in all things I have learned both to be full and to be hungry, both to abound and to suffer need. I can do all things through Christ who strengthens me.

Devotional:
In Philippians 4:11-13, the apostle Paul shares the secret of contentment—a contentment rooted not in circumstances but in the strength derived from God. It's a perspective that transcends financial highs and lows.

Reflection:
True financial contentment doesn't hinge on the magnitude of wealth we amass; rather, it resides in our reliance on God's unwavering provision and the resilience He imparts to navigate diverse circumstances. It's an understanding that transcends material abundance, emphasizing the profound peace that comes from trusting in a higher source. By anchoring our contentment in spiritual fortitude, we gain a perspective that allows us to find joy and security regardless of financial fluctuations, fostering a deeper connection to enduring sources of strength and fulfillment.

Daily Prayer
Heavenly Father, grant me humility in times of financial success. Help me remain grounded in Your truth and resist the allure of pride and arrogance. May I use my resources to bless others and advance Your kingdom.
In Jesus' name, I pray.
Amen.

What is your takeaway from these scriptures?

Journaling Prompts: Reflect on how you define financial contentment. In what ways has your definition been influenced by external circumstances? Consider Paul's journey of learning to be content in all situations.

How can you apply this perspective to your own financial journey? In what areas of your financial life do you need to rely more on God's strength? How can you actively seek His guidance and provision?

_____

_____

_____

_____

_____

_____

_____

_____

_____

_____

_____

_____

_____

_____

_____

_____

_____

_____

Life Application Reflection: Think about practical ways you can cultivate contentment in your financial life. This might involve setting realistic expectations, practicing gratitude, and actively trusting God's provision.

How can you apply this in your life?

_____
_____
_____
_____
_____

Closing Prayer

Heavenly Father,
I come before You with a heart brimming with gratitude for the abundant provision in my life. In the midst of the complexities, help me cultivate a spirit of contentment, appreciating the richness of Your blessings. Grant me the wisdom to find joy in the simplicity of what You've bestowed upon me, recognizing that true wealth lies not just in material possessions but in the depth of Your love and provision. May I embrace each day with a thankful heart, trusting in Your perfect plan for my life.
In Jesus' name, I pray.
Amen.

Practical Solution for a Financial Need

Christian Dating Coaching

Offer coaching services for Christian singles seeking guidance in their dating lives. Provide advice on faith-aligned relationships, helping individuals navigate the challenges of modern dating.

Week 50: Timeless Wisdom and Comfort

Date:

Bible Reading: Psalm 34:17-18
The righteous cry out, and the LORD hears, and delivers them out of all their troubles. The LORD is near to those who have a broken heart, and saves such as have a contrite spirit.

Devotional:
Psalm 34:17-18 offers reassurance that the righteous, in their moments of distress, find solace in the Lord. This passage underscores God's attentive ear to the cries of the brokenhearted and His salvation for those crushed in spirit. It stands as a comforting reminder that, even in the depths of hardship, God is intimately close, ready to hear and deliver those who turn to Him with a contrite heart.

Reflection:
In financial challenges, Psalm 34:17-18 serves as a source of comfort. It assures us of God's attentive ear to our cries and His nearness in moments of distress. This timeless wisdom becomes a reassuring anchor, affirming that even in the midst of financial struggles, the righteous find solace in the Lord. It encourages us to turn to Him with confidence, knowing that His salvation is readily available for those who seek refuge in the midst of financial trials.

Daily Prayer
Heavenly Father, surround me with godly mentors who can offer wisdom and guidance in financial matters. Help me learn from their experiences and seek counsel from those who walk in Your ways. May I grow in wisdom and discernment.
In Jesus' name, I pray.
Amen.

What is your takeaway from these scriptures?

Journaling Prompts: Reflect on your typical response when facing financial challenges. How can Psalm 34:17-18 shape your attitude and actions during difficult times?

In what ways can you actively draw near to God when facing financial difficulties? How might cultivating a spirit of prayer and dependence on Him strengthen your resolve?

_____
_____
_____
_____
_____
_____
_____
_____
_____
_____
_____
_____
_____
_____
_____

Life Application Reflection: Think about practical ways to anchor your trust in God during financial challenges. This might involve seeking support from a community of believers, and relying on biblical promises to find solace in difficult circumstances.

How can you apply this in your life?

_____

_____

_____

_____

_____

_____

_____

_____

_____

_____

_____

Closing Prayer

Heavenly Father, in times of financial challenges, I cry out to You. Hear my prayers and deliver me from troubles. Draw near to me as I navigate difficulties, and help me to trust in Your salvation. May my spirit find refuge in Your presence. In Jesus' name, I pray. Amen.

Practical Solution for a Financial Need

Virtual Christian Art Exhibitions

Organize virtual art exhibitions showcasing Christian artists.
Charge artists a fee to participate and allow them
to sell their artwork during the online event.
Or, create your own exhibition!

Week 51: Trusting God in Financial Uncertainty

Date:

Bible Reading: Psalm 23:1
The LORD is my shepherd; I shall not want.

Devotional:
Psalm 23:1 beautifully encapsulates the essence of trust in God's provision. It portrays the Lord as our caring shepherd, affirming that under His watchful care, we lack nothing. This declaration instills confidence in His boundless ability to meet our needs and navigate us through life's challenges. It's a timeless reminder that with God as our shepherd, we can rest assured in His provision, finding comfort and security in His unfailing care for every aspect of our lives.

Reflection:
In times of financial uncertainty, Psalm 23:1 becomes a reassuring anchor, emphasizing that our Shepherd is more than capable of guiding us through any challenges. This timeless verse becomes a source of comfort, instilling confidence in God's ability to navigate us through the complexities of financial uncertainties. It invites us to trust in His provision, finding solace in the knowledge that under His watchful care, we lack nothing essential for our well-being and flourishing.

Daily Prayer
Heavenly Father, bless me with creativity in finding solutions to financial challenges. Help me think outside the box and explore new opportunities.
May I trust in Your provision and step out in faith.
In Jesus' name, I pray. Amen.

What is your takeaway from this scripture?

Journaling Prompts: Reflect on your perception of God as your Shepherd. How can Psalm 23:1 deepen your trust in His provision, especially in financial uncertainties?

Consider moments when you've faced financial lack. How does the truth that the Lord is your Shepherd inspire confidence in His ability to provide?

Reflect on the statement, "I lack nothing." How can you actively trust in God's provision, even in the face of financial uncertainties?

_____
_____
_____
_____
_____
_____
_____
_____
_____
_____
_____
_____
_____
_____
_____
_____
_____

Life Application Reflection: Think about practical ways to deepen your trust in God's provision during financial uncertainties. This might involve increasing your reliance on prayer and seeking His guidance.

How can you apply this in your life?

_____
_____
_____
_____
_____
_____
_____

Closing Prayer

Heavenly Father,
in the midst of financial uncertainties, I lift my heart to You. You are my Shepherd, and I trust in Your provision. Grant me the strength to navigate challenges with faith, knowing that You are more than capable of guiding me through any uncertainties. Help me to lean on Your promises and find peace in the assurance that, under Your watchful care, I lack nothing essential.
In Jesus' name, I pray.
Amen.

Practical Solution for a Financial Need

Faith-Based Escape Room Experiences

Develop virtual or physical escape room experiences with Christian themes. Offer these experiences to churches, youth groups, or events, charging a fee for participation.

Week 52: Financial Accountability and Transparency

Date:

Bible Reading: Luke 16:10
"He who is faithful in what is least is faithful also in much; and he who is unjust in what is least is unjust also in much.

Devotional:
Luke 16:10 underscores the principle of financial accountability and transparency. This wisdom emphasizes the significance of faithfulness in managing resources, irrespective of their scale. It calls us to cultivate a spirit of integrity and responsibility in handling even the smallest aspects of our finances. This verse challenges us to recognize that our faithfulness in managing what may seem insignificant directly correlates with our ability to handle greater responsibilities in the realm of finances with trustworthiness and wisdom.

Reflection:
The foundational principle of financial stewardship, as highlighted in Luke 16:10, is being faithful with what we have, regardless of its size. This extends beyond mere management; it is a reflection of our character and trustworthiness. Recognizing the significance of even the smallest resources entrusted to us, this wisdom calls us to approach financial stewardship with integrity, understanding that our faithfulness in the little things paves the way for greater responsibilities.

Daily Prayer
Heavenly Father, grant me strength and perseverance to pursue financial goals with determination. Help me overcome obstacles and press forward with faith. May Your Spirit empower me to achieve greater heights in Your name. In Jesus' name, I pray. Amen.

What is your takeaway from this scripture?

Journaling Prompts: Reflect on your current approach to financial accountability. How do you manage even the smallest resources entrusted to you?

Consider the connection between trust and faithfulness in financial matters.

How does being faithful with little build a foundation for trust in handling more?

What practical steps can you take to enhance transparency in your financial dealings? How can you communicate your financial decisions with clarity and honesty?

_____
_____
_____
_____
_____
_____
_____
_____
_____
_____
_____
_____
_____
_____
_____
_____

Life Application Reflection: Think about practical ways to enhance financial accountability and transparency in your life. This might involve creating a budget, tracking expenses openly, and discussing financial decisions with accountability partners.

How can you apply this in your life?

_____
_____
_____
_____
_____
_____

Closing Prayer

Heavenly Father, guide me in being faithful with even the smallest resources You've entrusted to me. Help me to approach financial accountability with transparency and honesty. May my actions reflect a heart that can be trusted with both little and much. In Jesus' name, I pray. Amen.

Practical Solution for a Financial Need

Online Christian Book Club for Teens

Establish and moderate an in-person or virtual book club specifically tailored to teenagers, centered around Christian literature. Charge parents a subscription fee for teens to join and engage in meaningful discussions.

Conclusion: A Journey of Faith and Abundance

As you conclude this 52-Week Scripture-based prayer journal for financial breakthrough, you've embarked on a remarkable journey of faith, self-discovery, and transformation. This journey has been guided by the wisdom of the Bible, and it has been an opportunity to deepen your relationship with God and align your financial life with His purpose.

Throughout this prayer journal you've delved into the principles of trust, stewardship, generosity, and gratitude. You've sought God's guidance, surrendered your financial worries, and embraced His perfect plan for your finances. You've explored the significance of a compassionate heart and the joy of giving.

Financial breakthrough is not just about acquiring wealth; it's about experiencing a deeper, richer connection with God. It's recognizing that true abundance is found in His love and grace, and that your identity in Christ transcends worldly measures of success.

As you move forward, remember that your financial journey is a continual process of growth and learning. Embrace each day with a heart of gratitude, open to the blessings and lessons that God provides. Trust that your life is a testament to His goodness, and that by following His guidance, you are well on your way to a life of abundance, both spiritually and financially.

May you continue to find peace, joy, and contentment in your financial journey, and may you be a beacon of God's love and grace to others as you walk in faith.

With God, all things are possible. Continue to seek His presence, trust in His provision, and live a life marked by faith and abundance.

A Prayer For You

May the abundant life promised by our Heavenly Father
be your daily reality. May His love fill your heart with joy
and purpose. I pray for wisdom to navigate life's journey
and the strength to share His abundance with those around you.
May you be a beacon of grace, inspiring others
to embrace the fullness of life
rooted in God's love.

In Jesus' name, I pray these blessings upon you.
Amen.

Prayer Requests & Answers

Prayer Requests & Answers

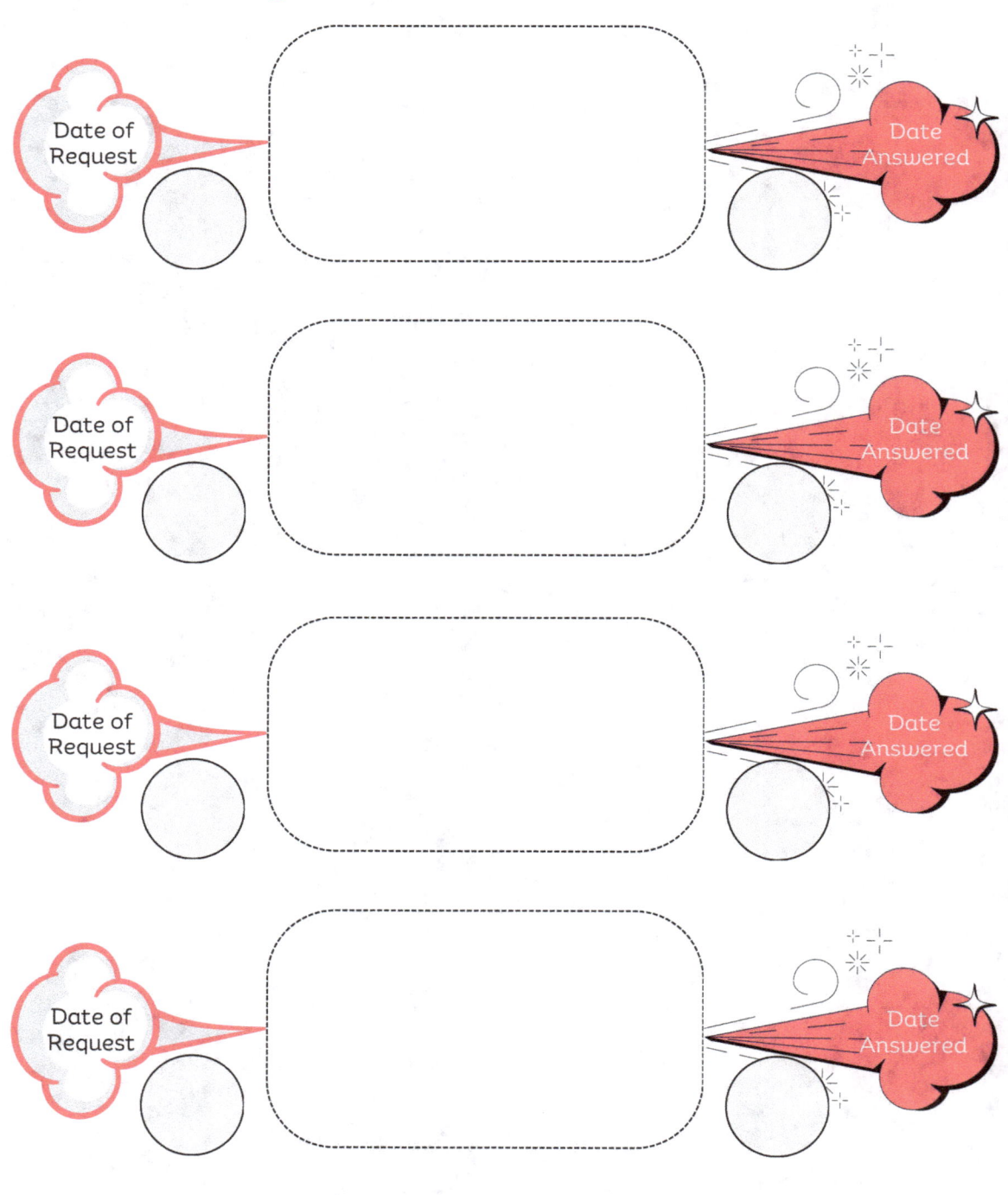

Prayer Requests & Answers

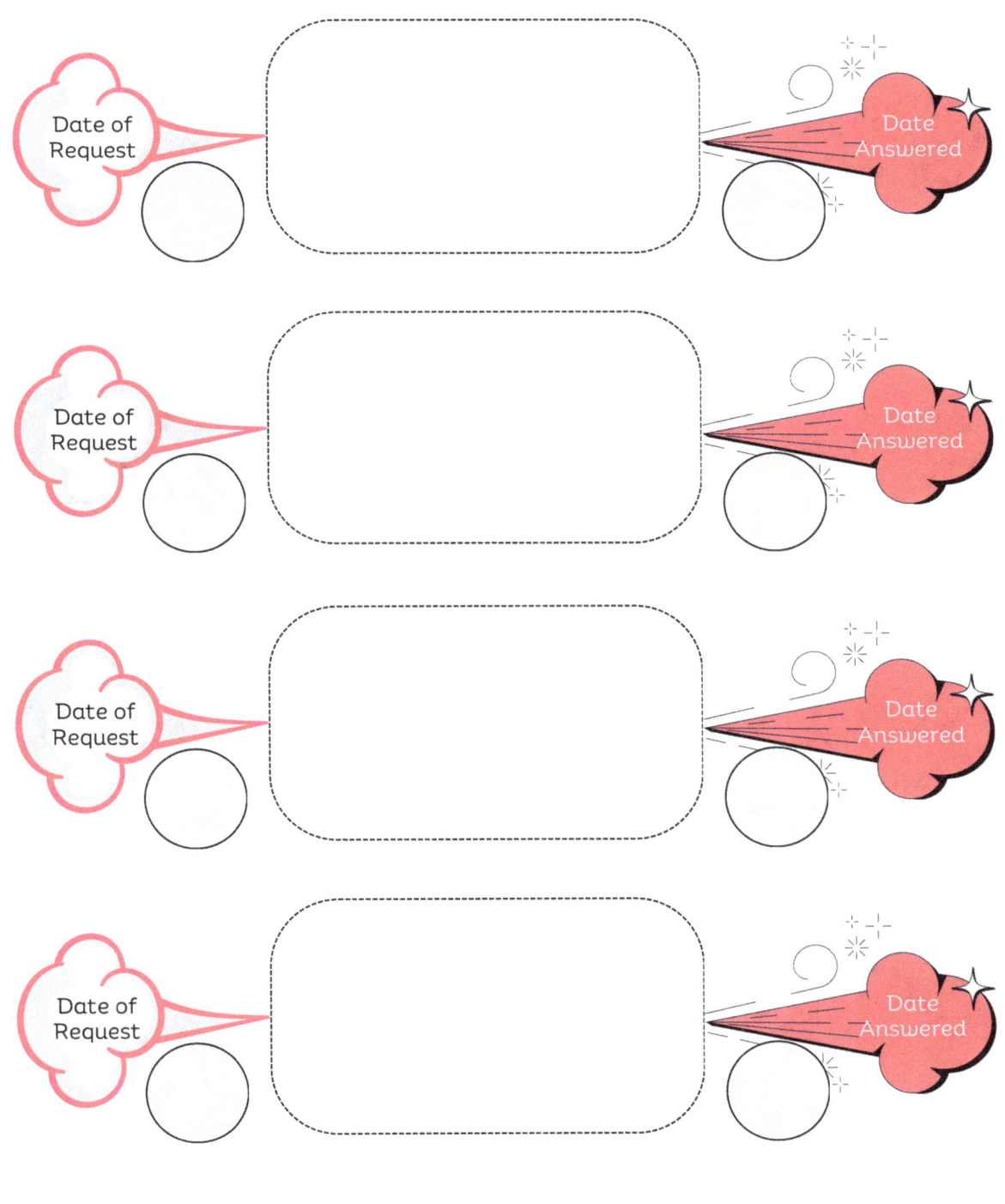

Prayer Requests & Answers

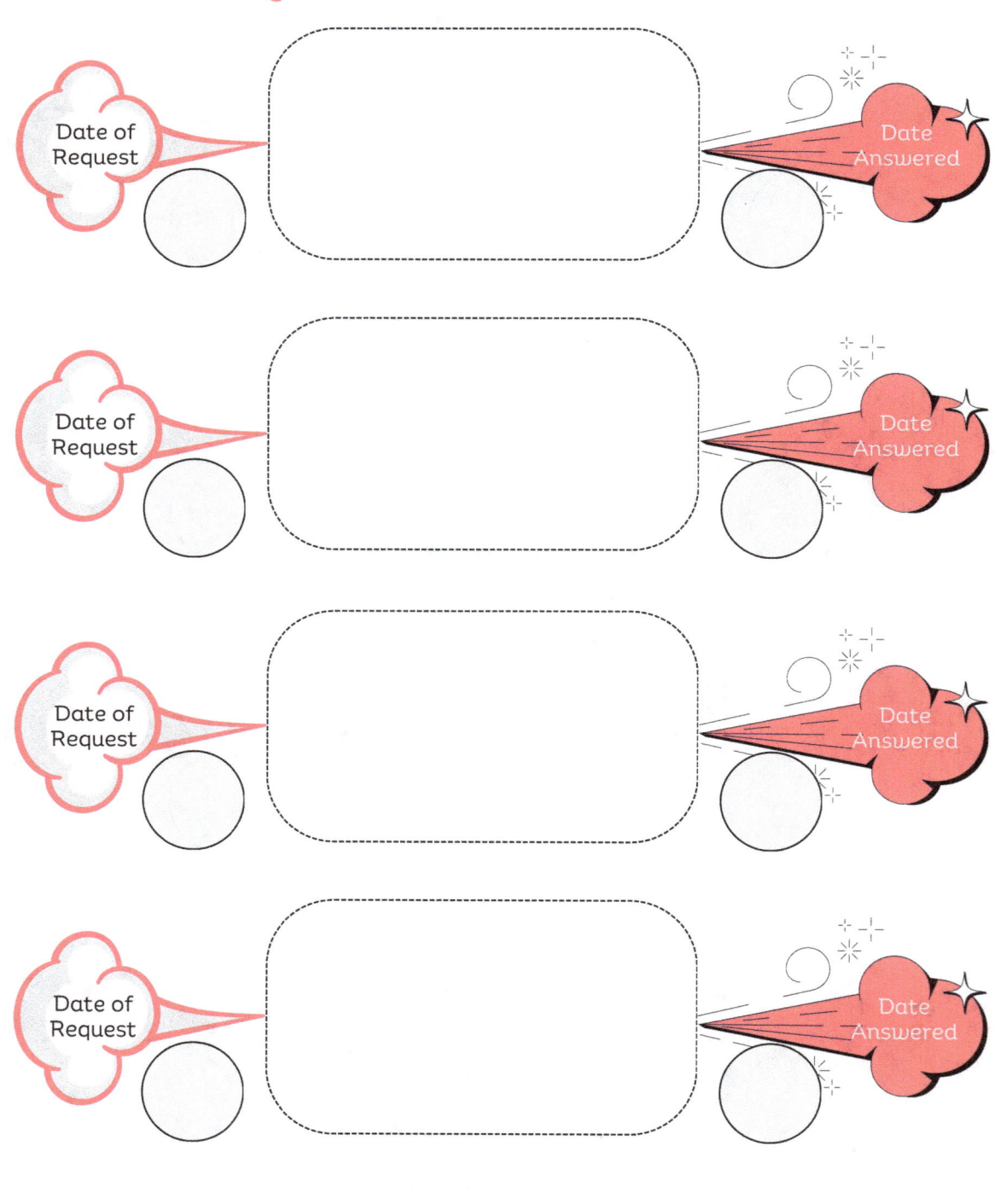

Prayer Requests & Answers

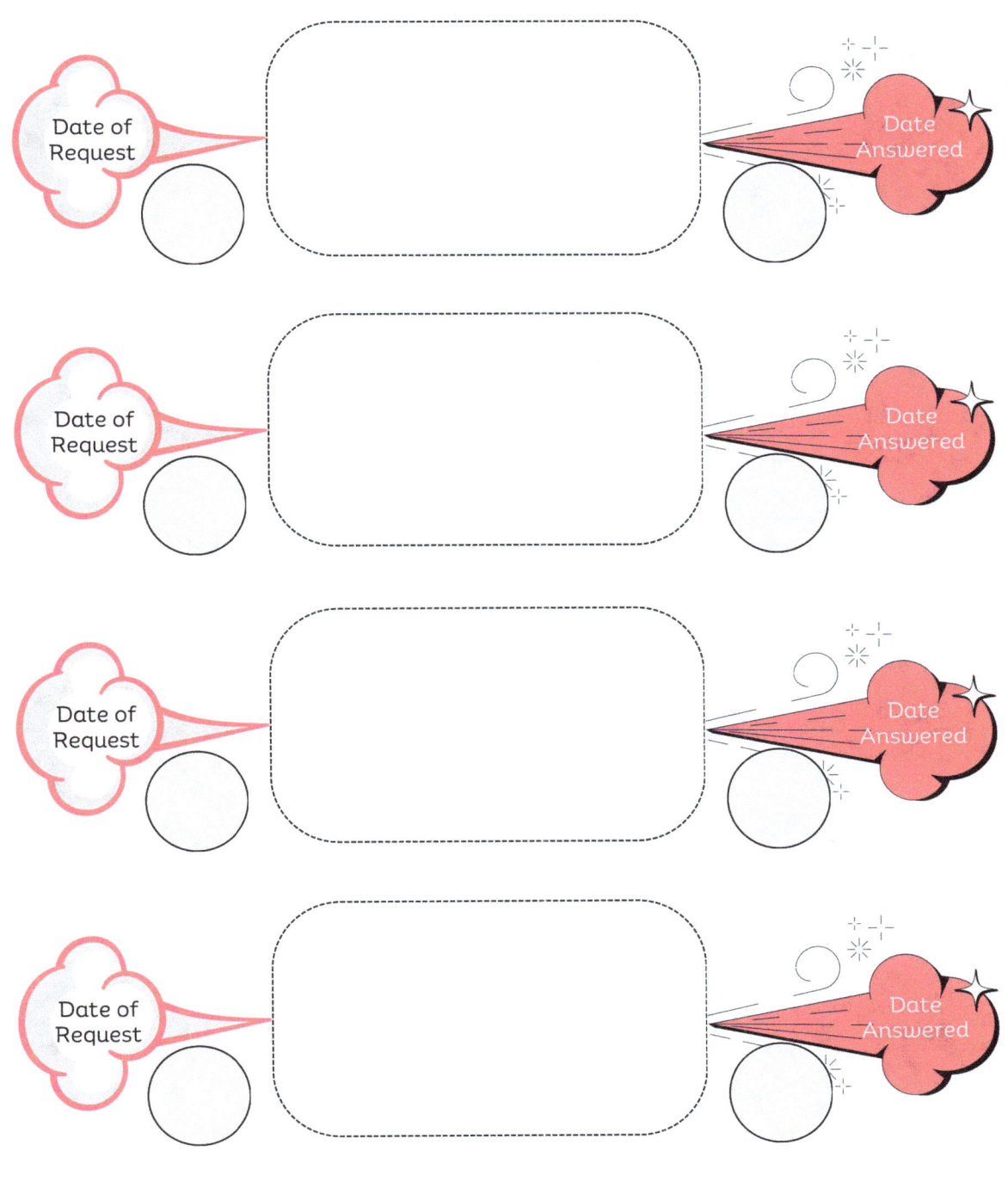

Prayer Requests & Answers

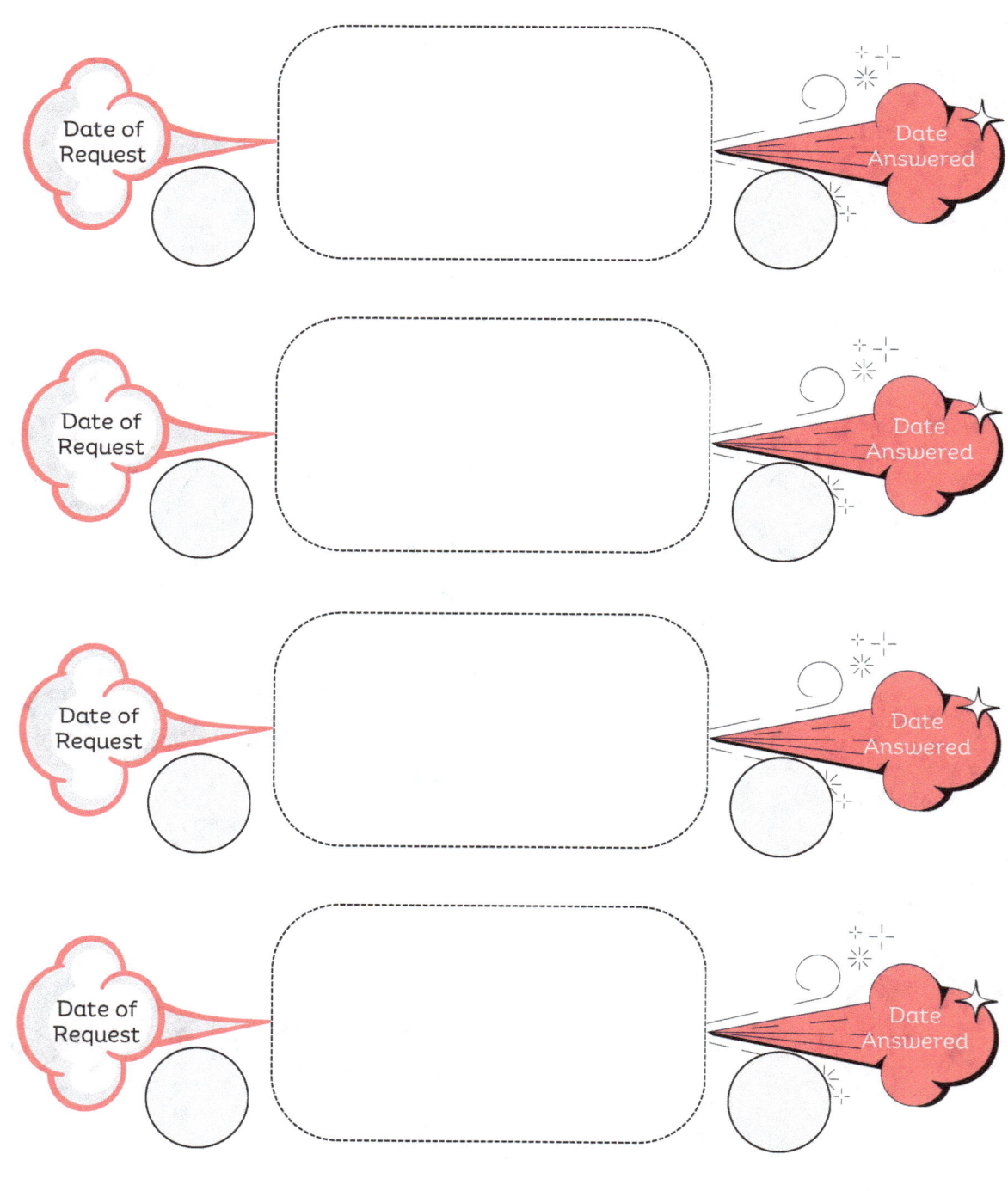

Prayer Requests & Answers

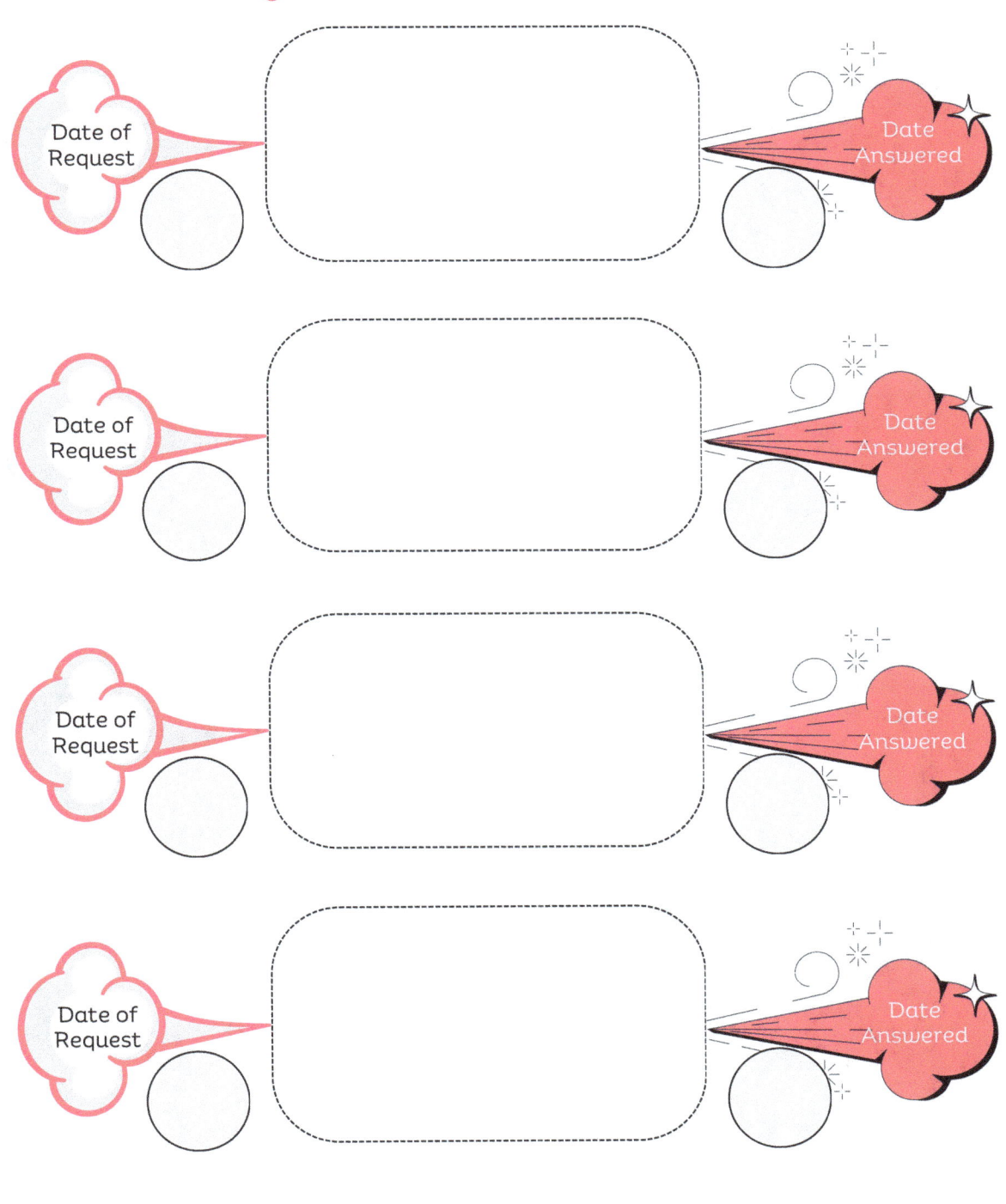

Prayer Requests & Answers

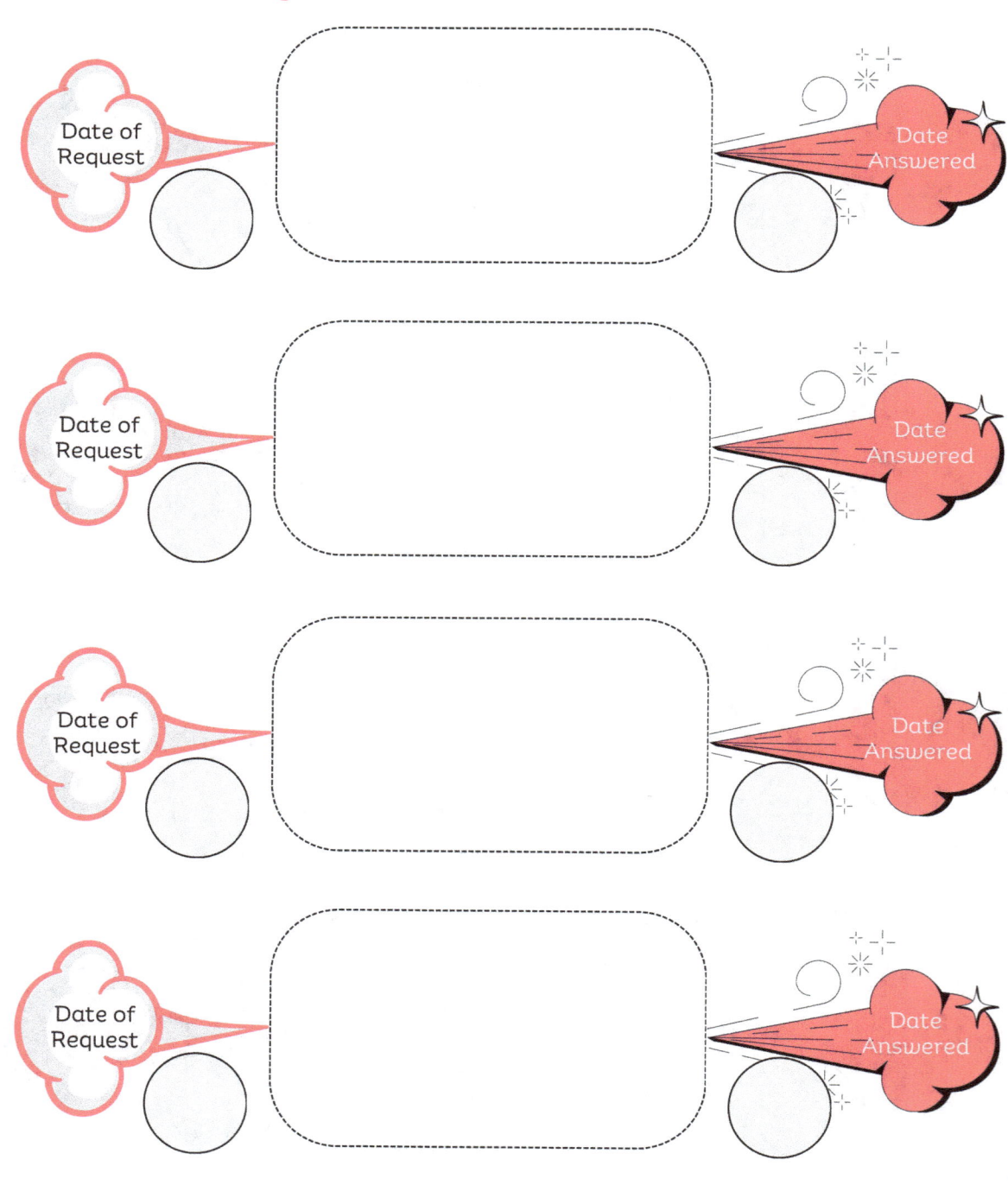

Prayer Requests & Answers

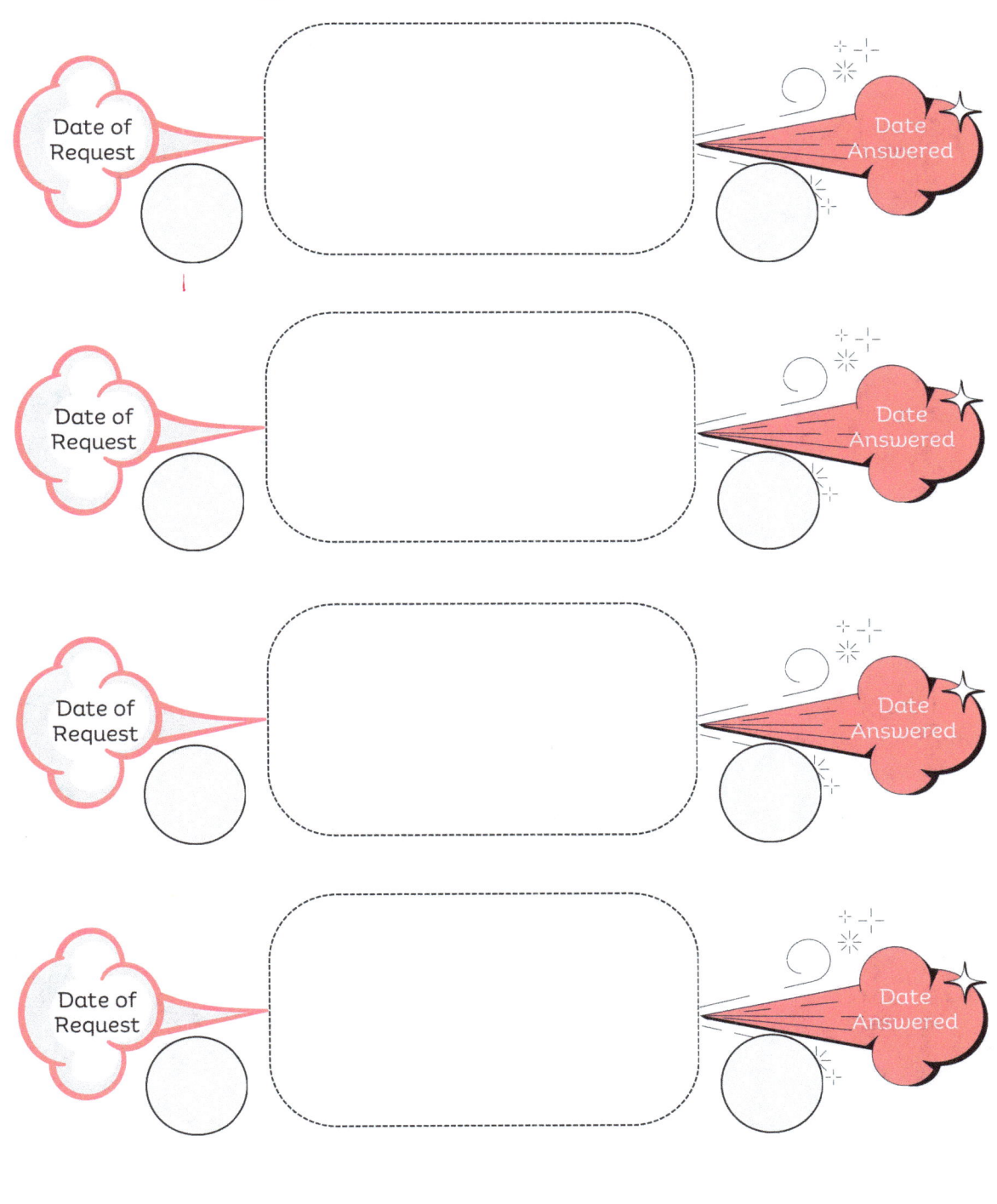

Prayer Requests & Answers

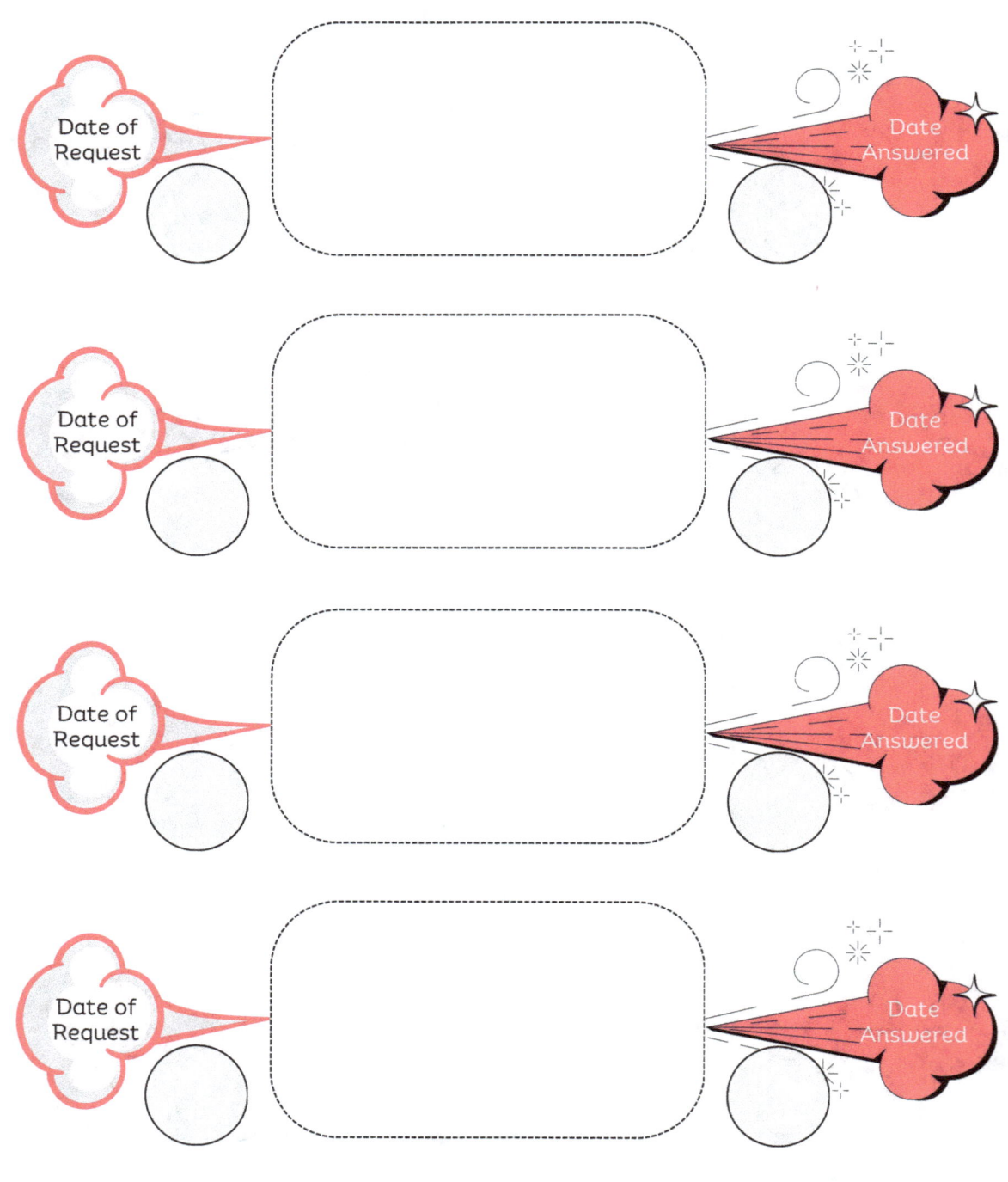

Prayer Requests & Answers

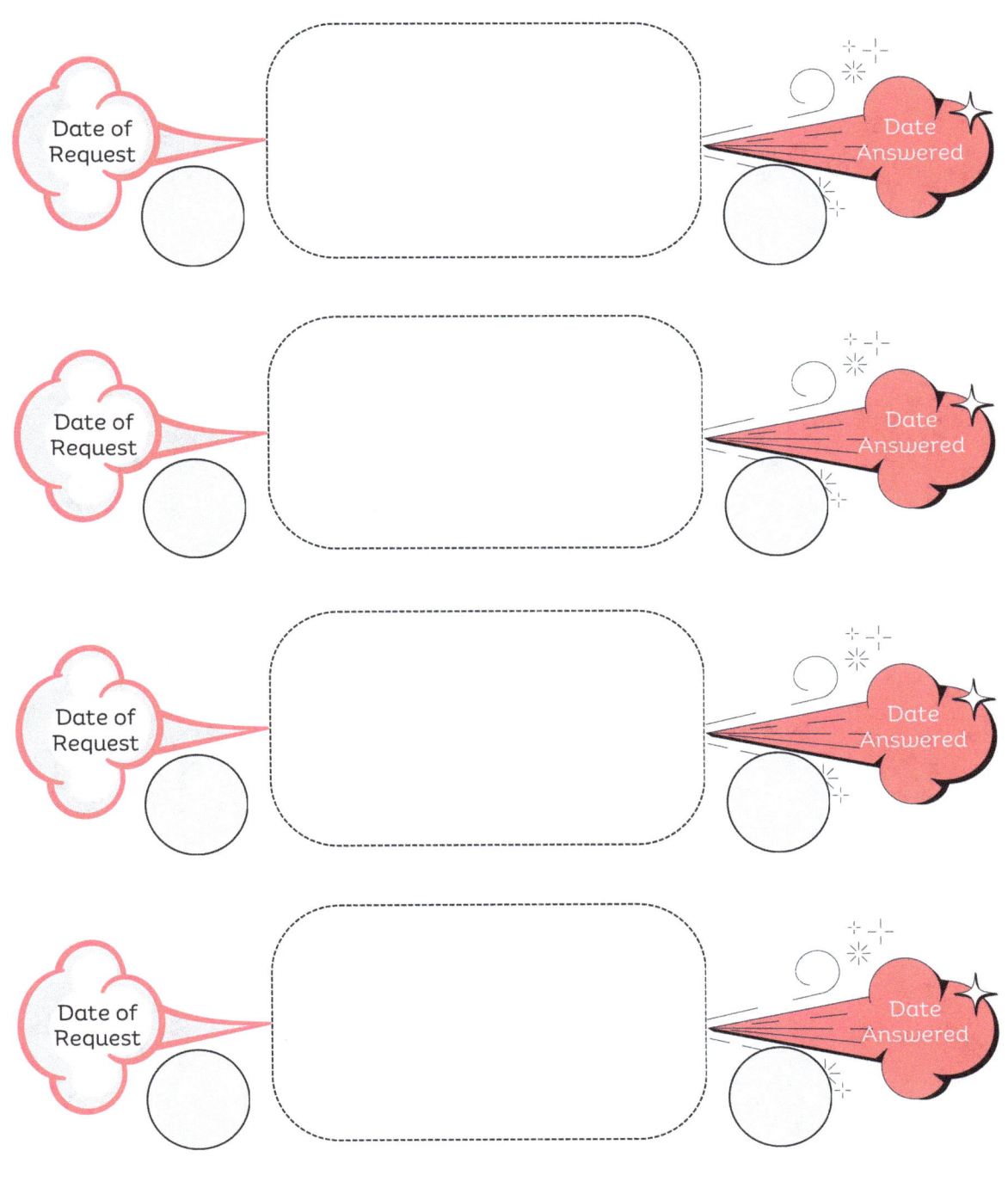

Prayer Requests & Answers

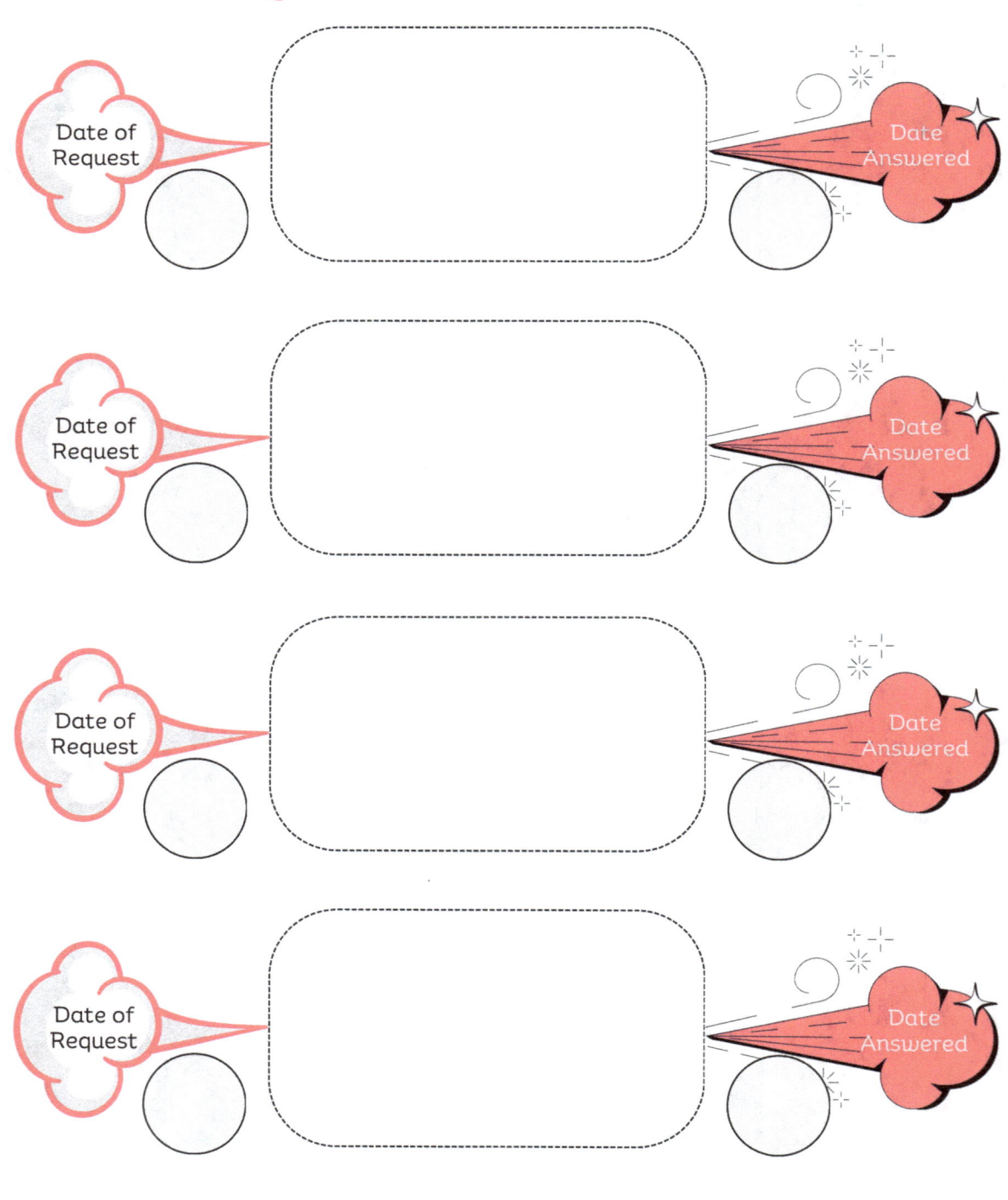

Prayer Requests & Answers

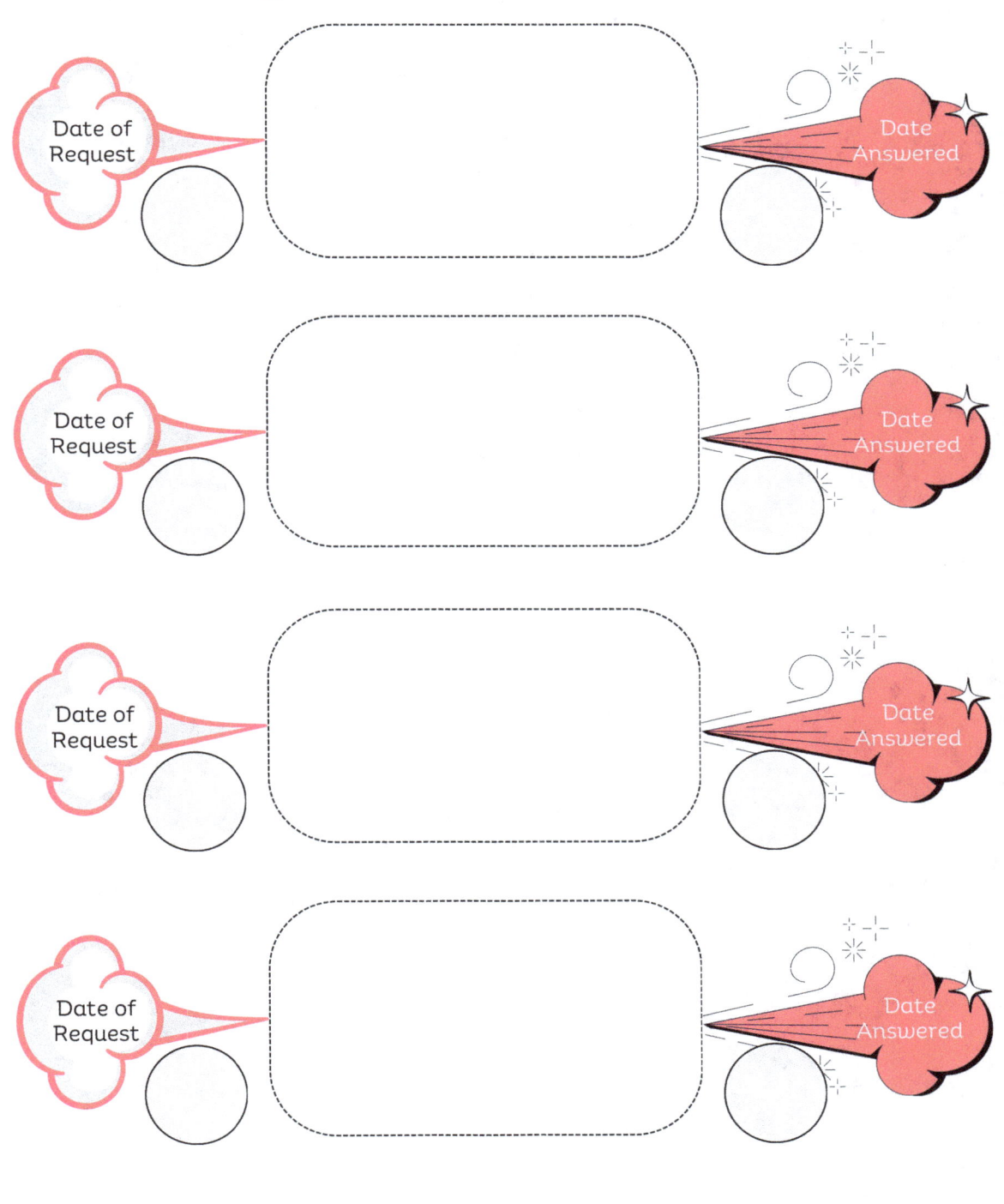

About the Author

Sincerely Shanene is a devoted mother of two grown children. She faced a life-altering moment when one of her kids battled cancer. In a selfless act of love, she retired from her advertising agency job to become a full-time stay-at-home mom, navigating both the emotional challenges and financial strains with unwavering strength.

Supported by her church community, she found solace and discovered a new path as she worked from home as a graphic designer, caring for her ailing child. The resilience she displayed during this period laid the foundation for the incredible journey that followed.

In just a few years, she founded a Christian publishing company, a testament to her determination and faith. This venture not only allowed her to fulfill her responsibilities as a single mom but also became a haven for aspiring writers. Her nurturing spirit has turned many first-time writers into bestselling authors, a source of immense joy for her.

Sincerely Shanene is grateful for the chance to be a conduit of God's grace, especially when she helps others share their stories and become published authors. She is currently focused on creating various items such as, home decor, wall art, gift wrap, apparel, journals, and books, all aimed at deepening your relationship with Christ. Moreover, she is working on turning screenplays into movies, and utilizing her musical talent for the kingdom of God.

Free Gift For You

Scan the QR Code to Download Your Free Gift.

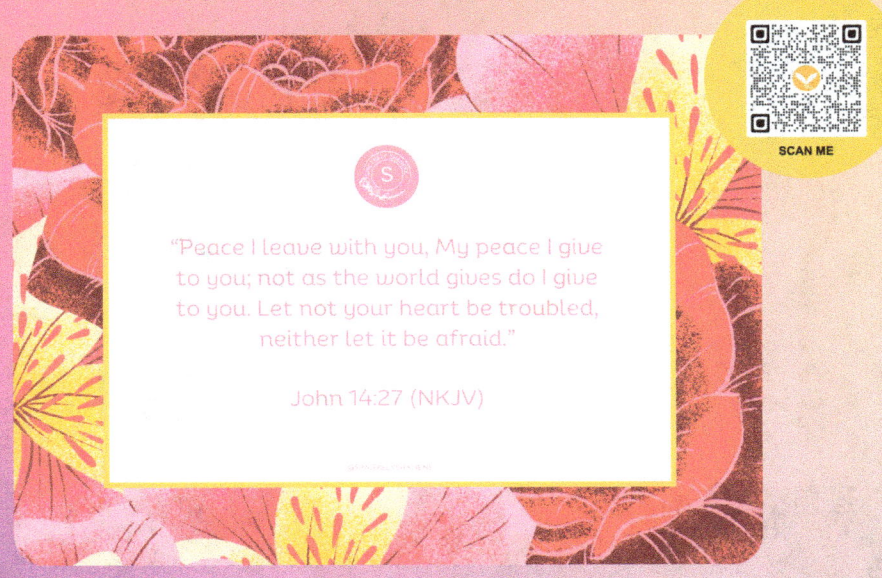

"Peace I leave with you, My peace I give to you; not as the world gives do I give to you. Let not your heart be troubled, neither let it be afraid."

John 14:27 (NKJV)

SCAN ME

Recommended Reads

Find at HigginsPublishing.com
Amazon, Barnes & Noble, and wherever books are sold!

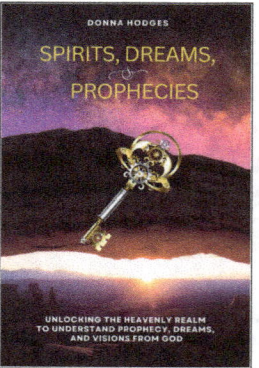

Thank you for supporting some of the authors that God has blessed me to publish!

If you found joy in using this Prayer Journal for Women,
I kindly invite you to share your thoughts by leaving a review on Amazon
or the platform where you made your purchase.

Your feedback means a lot to me, and I'd love to hear how this journal
has been a source of help and inspiration for you.

Thank you for taking a moment to review this journal!

Now to Him who is able to do exceedingly abundantly above
all that we ask or think, according to the power that works in us,
to Him be glory in the church by Christ Jesus
to all generations, forever and ever.
Amen.

Ephesians 3:20-21

www.ingramcontent.com/pod-product-compliance
Lightning Source LLC
Chambersburg PA
CBHW081442070526
44586CB00019B/2205